BRITISH SCHOOL OF ARCHAEOLOGY IN EGYPT

ELEVENTH YEAR

SAQQARA MASTABAS

PART II

BY

MARGARET A. MURRAY

WITH CHAPTERS BY

PROFESSOR KURT SETHE

AND DRAWINGS BY F. HANSARD, HILDA PETRIE, AND F. KINGSFORD

HISTORIES & MYSTERIES OF MAN LTD.

LONDON, ENGLAND

1989

Printed in U.S.A.

Further Titles in Series include:

I) BALLAS by J.E. Quibell
II) The RAMESSEUM by J.E. Quibell & The Tomb of PTAH-HETEP by F.LL. Griffith
III) EL KAB by J.E. Quibell
IV) HIERAKONPOLIS I by J.E. Quibell
V) HIERAKONPOLIS II by F.W. Green and J.E. Quibell
VI) EL ARABAH by J. Garstang
VII) MAHASNA by J. Garstang
VIII) TEMPLE OF THE KINGS AT ABYDOS by A.St.G. Caulfield
IX) The OSIREION by Margaret Alice Murray
X) SAQQARA MASTABAS I by Margaret Alice Murray

ANCIENT RECORDS OF EGYPT by James Henry Breasted
ANCIENT RECORDS OF ASSYRIA by David Luckenbill
ANCIENT EGYPTIAN MATERIALS AND INDUSTRIES by A. Lucas
HYKSOS & ISRAELITE CITIES Double Volume by Petrie & Duncan
THE CHRONOLOGY OF ANCIENT KINGDOMS AMENDED by Sir Isaac Newton
SAQQARA MASTABAS II by Margaret Alice Murray
STONEHENGE by Petrie. Updated by Gerald Hawkins

For further details please write for catalogue to
HISTORIES & MYSTERIES OF MAN LTD.
The Glassmill
1, Battersea Bridge Road
London SW11 3BG
ENGLAND

ISBN 1 854 17 043 0

BRITISH SCHOOL OF ARCHAEOLOGY IN EGYPT

CONTENTS

This volume is the eleventh memoir of the series, referring to work in 1904 and 1905.

LIST OF PLATES

SAQQARA MASTABAS

PART II

INTRODUCTION.

1. This volume contains the important translations by Professor Kurt Sethe of the inscriptions in *Saqqara Mastabas* I. His MS was not finished till after that volume had appeared. It has remained unpublished awaiting the publication of the second volume, and during the interval the illustrious author has passed away. This volume is therefore the poorer in not having his corrections of the MS and the proofs. The only alterations I have made in his work are in the transliterations where newer and more accurate forms have been discovered—often by Professor Sethe himself—since his three chapters were written. The plate references in Professor Sethe's chapters are to volume I.

The drawings from the tomb of Ty were made by Lady Petrie, Miss Hansard (Mrs. Firth), and Miss Kingsford (Lady Cockerell). These were made before the publication of the tomb by Professor Steindorff, but it was considered advisable to publish them here on a sufficiently large scale for detailed study.

For the same reason the figure of Seker-kha-bau is republished on a large scale. Miss Hansard's careful drawing of the necklace was the first indication to me of the importance of that priestly ornament. So little is known about any of the early deities that I have thought it worth while to make a short study of a few of those mentioned in the Saqqara tombs published in volume I, and in the forthcoming volume *Seven Memphite Tomb Chapels* copied by Lady Petrie and her staff.

CHAPTER I.

ANUBIS.

2. In *Saqqara Mastabas* I the false door of Seker-kha-bau is reproduced on too small a scale to permit of the collar or necklace being seen in full detail. As this ornament appears to be part of the official insignia of the priesthood, it seemed worth while to reproduce the upper part of the figure of Seker-kha-bau on a sufficiently large scale for careful study (Pl. I).

Besides the collar there are a few points which are worth noting. Though the wife of Seker-kha-bau has the same short-nosed type of face as Zoser, the man himself is not only unlike her but is also unlike any other portraits of officials surviving from the IIIrd and IVth dynasties. The big, rather aquiline, nose, the large projecting lips and the short chin combine to give a sinister cast of countenance which resembles the portrait of Sa-nekht (Petrie, *Researches in Sinai*, pl. 48), and shows that this is truly a likeness and not a conventionalised representation of a priest of high rank. The likeness between Seker-kha-bau and Sa-nekht is sufficiently close as to suggest a blood relationship between the two.

For the description of the dress see vol. I, p. 3. The wig must, I think, have had as its foundation a close-fitting cloth cap on which the twists of hair were sewn. There are three lengths of these twists; the longest falls from the crown of the head to the top of the ear, the next row is about the length of the ear, and the shortest comes from the lower part of the ear to the nape of the neck. (For the method of arranging a wig of this kind, see M. Gauthier Laurent in *Mélanges Maspero*, p. 85 *seq.*)

The most important item of the dress is, however, the collar. Though this is a very early period of Egyptian art, the collar is an example of that stylization which was the curse of the Egyptian artist; and it represents in a highly conventionalised form a much earlier and more primitive object. It consists of two parts, one lying over the other. The under portion is evidently made of some rigid material such as metal, possibly gold. It is held round the neck of the wearer by a ring; attached to the ring are three bars shaped like the zigzag sign for water; the middle bar runs down vertically, the two side bars flare out to right and left respectively. At their lower ends the three bars are fastened to a curved bar. At the side of the junction of the right and left bars with the curved bar is a knob. I suggest that in the original object the knob was a knot, and that the bar was perhaps a cord of some kind ; or, if it were originally made of a rigid material, that the knot was part of the string which tied the zigzag to the curved bar. The central zigzag ends in a ring, which I suggest was originally a ring-amulet of fibre or string, of the kind found in later times. The knobs and ring project beyond the curved bar of which they are here represented as forming part.

The curved bar appears to belong to the zigzags and to have had no original connection with the continuation on each side of the curve. This continuation is so formed as to represent the figure of Anubis, the head at one shoulder of the wearer, the tail at the other. Like all early figures of jackals, the body is exaggeratedly thin. The animal is represented with two human arms, of which the hands are held near the snout, in what is possibly an attitude of adoration. (Cf. the gesture with that of Neheb-ka, also an early deity.) Lower down the body are two feet so entirely stylized that they would be unrecognisable as feet if detached from the body. The animal is thus complete—with head, body and four limbs, though without a tail—on one side of the ornament. On the other side is the body of a jackal with four feet and a tail but without a head. The ornament is so conventionalised and altered from its earliest form that it is impossible to say whether there were originally two jackals, one on each side ; or whether there was but one slung across the chest of the wearer with the head pointing to one shoulder, the tail to the other. The little hind-legs immediately under the tail seem to show, by their size and position, that they were originally part of the tail and that the maker of the collar had misunderstood their meaning. The late forms studied by Erman (*Z.A.S.*, 1894, pp. 18 *seq.*) show that in the New Kingdom there was only one jackal across the priest's chest. Owing to the limitations of relief-sculpture, it is uncertain whether this part of the necklace was cut out of sheet metal, i.e. was flat, or whether the figure of the jackal was modelled in relief or in the round.

The second part of the necklace which overlay, and was distinct from, the stiff bars consists of twelve strings hung round the neck. The strings are graduated in length, and on each is slung a single pendant. On the first three are *ankhs*, the next three hold disks, then come three more *ankhs*, and lastly three disks ; six *ankhs* and six disks in all. The *ankhs* are threaded through the oval loop which is an integral part of the sign, the disks have a ring at the top through which the string passes ; the ring shows that the object is not a bead, and the circular hollow in the centre indicates that it is a disk, not a ball.

The significance of this remarkable ornament has never attracted much attention. It has been suggested, and the suggestion has been generally accepted, that it was part of the insignia of the High Priest of Memphis. I am, however, of the opinion that this is not the true explanation. The principal arguments against it are : (1) that the ornament is excessively rare, whereas the number of known High Priests of Memphis is relatively great, especially in the Old Kingdom ; and (2) that Seker-kha-bau, though he uses the title of *sekhem hemti* (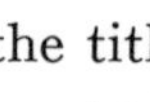) has not the full title which betokens the High Priest. It seems, then, that the ornament, in the Old Kingdom at any rate, must refer to some other priesthood, and the importance in it of the jackal strongly suggests a priesthood of Anubis.

3. Anubis is a god of whom very little is known. No special locality or district belongs to him and therefore no temple is dedicated to his sole worship, though he occasionally has chapels built in his honour in the temple of some other god. His function is that of Death ; he has not, like Osiris or Seker, any connection with the life after death ; he is Death personified. He is an early deity, and as such he belonged originally to the Pharaoh alone. Like all primitive deities he has no consort, and till late times he stands alone without any connection with other gods or goddesses. His inclusion in the Osirian Cycle is not only late but too vague to be convincing.

The standard of Anubis was one of the earliest of the royal standards, and was carried before the King in the earliest times of which there is any record. On the mace-heads of the Scorpion King and of Narmer, his standard comes next to the emblem of birth, thus symbolizing the beginning and end of the royal life.

The position of Anubis in regard to the rest of the Egyptian pantheon has never been accurately studied ; he has been called the God of Death, and that is all. I therefore venture to make here a few suggestions.

The clearest classification of the Egyptian

pantheon which has yet been made is by PETRIE (*Religion and Conscience*, p. 68 *seq.*). I use it as the basis of my argument, though with some modifications, arranged thus :—

1. *Local deities.* Usually animal or animal-headed. These are probably the most primitive deities.

2. *The Osiris Cycle.* The dogmas of the Osirian worship were not fully established till the New Kingdom. Even so late as the Pyramid Texts, Seth is the friend and helper of Osiris. The original Osirian group consisted of Osiris, Isis and Nephthys only ; Seth, Horus and Anubis are late additions.

3. *The Royal Gods.* Here the continual changes in the Kingship must be taken into account. The sun, which was so essentially the royal deity in the New Kingdom, is unknown in the early periods. This fact is clearly shown by the royal names which (with the exception of Neferka-Ra) are never compounded with Ra till the IVth dynasty. The legend of the birth of the Kings of the Vth dynasty indicates the introduction of sun-worship and shows that it was peculiar to the royal family.

In following out the development of the Egyptian religion it must be remembered that that religion was never static, and that democratization is an influence to be reckoned with. The ideas and dogmas originally belonging only to the King spread gradually to the higher ranks of the nobles, thence to the lesser officials, and finally permeated all classes. The Osirian dogmas are a good instance of the democratization of an idea. The contrast between the Pyramid Texts and the Book of the Dead is also worth noting ; the one being for Kings only, the other for the generality of mankind. Unfortunately, in studying the religion, the greater number of Egyptologists have been influenced by the classical authors and late texts, and have not realised the changes which took place in the long course of Egyptian religion. The consequent result is that Ra is regarded now as having been always the supreme deity of Egypt. But in the proto-dynastic period, to which Seker-kha-bau belonged, the pantheon, particularly the early gods, were very different from those of a later time. There is reason to believe that in the early religion the deities, other than the local gods, belonged to the Kings only. A local god or goddess was worshipped by the people of the district which he or she governed, but deities like Anubis or Heqt, who had no local status and therefore no temple, were special deities belonging only to the Pharaoh, the incarnate God. Our knowledge of the Egyptian religion is still so fragmentary that it is essential to study the early gods singly and in detail. Till this has been done adequately and from an anthropological point of view, the Egyptian religion will remain to modern eyes entirely formless and static.

Besides the god Seker, whose name is compounded in the personal name, only four other divinities are mentioned in the inscriptions of Seker-kha-bau ; these are Anubis, Seth, Seshat, and the fetish of the Oxyrhynchus nome. Of the last nothing is known ; the drawing of the object, which possibly represents the name of the local god, gives no clue to its real meaning. Yet it was obviously divine, as Seker-kha-bau was its priest.

Of Seth so much was written by Plutarch and others that the position and attributes of the god have been completely obscured, and that obscurity has been increased by many of the authors of modern books on Egyptian religion. The position of Seth in early times is clearly indicated in the Pyramid Texts of Pepy and Merenra (see *Ancient Egypt*, 1928, p. 8 *seq.*), where Seth is the Giver of Fertility and is sacrificed for the good of his people, an aspect not generally recognised by the writers on Egyptian religion. [Seth was god of the Anu.—F. P.]

In the case of Anubis the confusion arose, as with Seth, in that confused period, the New Kingdom, when new and foreign ideas began to infiltrate into the more primitive cults. The theologians, probably the priests of Heliopolis which was the centre of all theology and speculative religion, re-arranged the pantheon, paired off the deities who had no consorts (e.g. Ptah with Sekhmet), or invented goddesses for bachelor gods (e.g. Amont and Amon). They also identified one deity with another, like Sekhmet and Bast, though originally the two were quite distinct. The sun's journey through the other world is another example of the theological attempt to fuse unconnected ideas together ; here the priests sent the sun through the other worlds of various parts of Egypt ; the clumsiness of the arrangement is seen by the fact that the morning star, heralding the dawn, appears three times in the course of the night's journey.

The identification of one god with another is responsible for the confusion which existed in late times between the two jackal gods, Anubis the god of Death, and Wep-wawut, the local god of Siut. The confusion between the two is most marked from the New Kingdom onwards, though it began earlier ; but even in the Middle Kingdom Wep-wawut was not the same as Anubis ; he had his temple at Siut and functioned within his own district, whereas Anubis belonged to every part of Egypt.

4. The priestly insignia of Seker-kha-bau so obviously refer to Anubis that it is worth while to examine the priestly titles in the inscriptions. Of the four deities mentioned, Seker-kha-bau is prophet 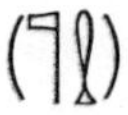 of Seshat and of the fetish of Oxyrhynchus, and he holds the rare title of  in the cult of Seth ; for the worship of each of these three deities he holds one title only. But for the cult of Anubis he holds two offices ; consequently it is only logical to infer that he was an important personage in the service of that god. The priesthoods occur in a group together on the back of the false door, on one of the side panels, and on the lintel. On the other side panel there are civilian titles only, with the exception of the priesthood of Seshat ; and on the drum there are again only civilian titles.

The two priestly titles referring to Anubis are *mḏḥ İnpw ḫnti t' ḏśr* " Builder (lit. axe-man) of Anubis, Chief of the Sacred Land " ; and *ḥḳ' n sḥ nṯr İnpw* " Ruler of the divine shrine of Anubis ". Both are rare titles. I cannot agree with Professor Sethe (see below, p. 11) in dividing the second title into two parts, as the division leaves the epithet of Anubis unconnected with any priesthood. Arranged as I have given it, the title makes good sense. Sethe bases his reading on the sealing in the tomb of Neterkhet (GARSTANG, *Mahasna*, pl. viii, 1) ; but in my opinion the word there reads *Uty*, as he himself suggested, this being an epithet of the god. In the early jar-sealings the name or figure of a deity is often set vertically between enclosed names of kings (PETRIE, *Royal Tombs*, pl. xxii, 179 ; GARSTANG, *Mahasna*, pl. ix, 5*a*, where the god's name is 'Ash, not Hor-akhti).

The two priestly titles are not only rare—the axe-man title is known only in the Old Kingdom when wooden architecture was in use—but the combination with Anubis is unique in the case of the axe-man, and the *Ruler of the Anubis shrine* occurs in only one other tomb, that of Y-em-hotep (L. *D.* ii, 113*e*).

5. In the present state of our knowledge of Egyptian burial customs it is impossible to say whether the peasants received burial in the Sacred Land, or whether that area was reserved for nobles only. If the former were the case, the burials found in any given cemetery must have consisted almost entirely of peasants, as the peasantry always greatly outnumber the nobility in any country. Yet the records of any modernly excavated cemetery, e.g. Saqqara, show that this was not the case. If, on the other hand, the peasantry did not practise inhumation, what became of the bodies? The scarcity of timber in Egypt precluded cremation ; the sand dries but does not destroy the corpses ; the only alternatives would be the river with its crocodiles, or exposure to birds and beasts of prey. The jackal and the vulture are the most prompt and active of such scavengers on dry land, the crocodile being equally prompt and active in the water ; and it is noticeable that all three creatures were deified. The reason for identifying the jackal more than the other two with death can only be surmised. I suggest that the reasons were that it is a nocturnal animal, and that it is also extremely liable to rabies, which last would make it a terror in the eyes of the people. Anyone who has lived in a country where mad jackals are not uncommon will understand the panic which they inspire. A rabid jackal will attack a human being with ferocity and, owing to the carrion on which it lives, its bite is often fatal even when the creature is not diseased. The combination of nocturnal habits and of almost certainly fatal bites would make the jackal an obvious emblem of death. Another fact which in Egypt connects the jackal with death is its habit of sitting on the tombs.

As death is the inevitable end of every life, it seems strange, at first sight, that the King should have a special God to bring that end to him. But if no King were ever allowed to die a natural death, an executioner must have been appointed when the allotted span of the royal life had run. In all places where the divine King is put to death, the sacrifice can only be consummated at the hands of a specially appointed priest ; otherwise to kill the King is worse than murder. The tribes of the Nilotic Sudan have, until recent times, practised the custom of sacrificing their incarnate Gods, and in every country where the rite is practised the victim is warned beforehand and an official executioner performs the sacrifice. BRUCE (*Travels to discover the Sources of the Nile*, iv, 459 seq., ed. 1790) makes this quite clear: "There is one officer of his (i.e. the King's) family who alone can be the instrument of shedding his sovereign and kinsman's blood . . . nor is any guilt imputed to him however many of his sovereigns he has thus murdered." This statement explains two facts connected with Anubis. The first is that when the name is determined with the sign of a child it means a prince or princess, in other words one of the King's own family; and second, that in the New Kingdom and later, Anubis is credited with being the son of Osiris, and according to Erman (*Z.A.S.*, 1910, p. 93 seq.) the name Osiris may mean the Occupier of the Throne. If, then, Anubis was the appointed messenger of death and possibly the executioner of the divine victim, his place in the pantheon of royal gods becomes clear; he is the death-god of the King. Such a suggestion is substantiated by the customs of the Shilluk, where, until the very end of the last century, the *ororo* or king-killer was always a member of the royal family, and also announced to the King that his time had come (SELIGMAN, *Pagan Tribes of the Nilotic Sudan*, p. 91). In other words, the Shilluk kept up the Anubis custom till modern times.

The significance of Seker-kha-bau's collar lies in the combination of Anubis and the number of *ankh*-signs. If my theory is correct and Anubis was the messenger to announce death to the predestined victim and to consummate the sacrifice, masking would probably be part of the ritual. I have already pointed out (*Ancient Egypt*, 1928, p. 8) that the Pyramid Texts of Pepy and Merenra show that the King was sacrificed as a fertility victim. As the Pyramid Texts were already corrupt from centuries of copying and as they also indicate to the King a way of escape from his fate, it is evident that the custom was even then extremely ancient.

Frazer has proved that the sacrifice was often consummated at the end of a term of years, usually seven or nine. The story of Menkaure shows that in Egypt the length of the term was seven years. The story is recorded by Herodotus (Book ii, 133). Menkaure, a Pharaoh of the IVth dynasty, was warned by an oracle of Buto that he would reign for six years and die in the seventh. As an oracle when first given has always to be interpreted by the priests, there is confirmation of the story in the account by Diodorus (iii, 6, 3) of Ergamenes, a king of Ethiopia, who was told by the priests that his hour had come. He had no intention of being sacrificed, he therefore assembled his soldiers, marched on the temple and killed the priests. In the case of Ergamenes the priests had decided on his death on account of his showing the first signs of old age, but the story of Menkaure indicates that in ancient Egypt a term was set to the reign, and that this term was seven years. There are two confirmations of this story. In a sculptured scene in the temple of Ne-user-re, of the Vth dynasty, Anubis presents the Pharaoh with seven *ankhs*, thus symbolizing the seven years of life then being allotted to the monarch. It should be noted that in the IVth dynasty Menkaure had six years of life and died in the seventh, while in the Vth dynasty Ne-user-re had seven complete years of life. A case parallel with Menkaure is that of Tut-ankh-Amon, who also was preceded by a blasphemous King, "the criminal of Akhetaten," but himself returned to the old religion and its rites and customs; he reigned six years and died in the seventh. Again, in the XXVIth dynasty, according to Herodotus (Book ii, 161), "Psammis reigned only six years over Egypt, and made an expedition into Ethiopia, and shortly afterwards died."

It seems, then, that the custom of sacrificing the royal god at the end of a term of years was known in Egypt from an early period. When the custom relaxes, the King can be represented by a substitute; this was probably the case in Egypt in the greater number of reigns, and it was only for certain Kings that the law was enforced. The rigorous insistence on the death of Menkaure may have been due to the fact that his two immediate predecessors, Khufu and Khafra, had "closed the temples and forbidden the sacrifices". If the sacrifices included the killing of the royal and divine victim, the action of the two Kings is quite understandable, but the action of the priests on the accession of a pious and retrogressive Pharaoh is equally understandable; they insisted on the fulfilment of the religious law after the lawlessness of the two previous impious monarchs. The "criminality" of Akhenaten may have been of the same type as that of Khufu and Khafra, and his successor paid the same penalty as the successor of the impious Kings of the IVth dynasty.

Anubis was the personification of Death, and it was therefore appropriate that he should indicate to Ne-user-re the length of life allotted to the King. His priest, masked with a jackal's head, was the dread messenger announcing the immediate approach of the final scene. The summoner, who called the incarnate God to become the chief god of the next world, had no temple, for there was, then as now, no means of propitiating death. Prayers and sacrifices cannot placate the King of Terrors, " mortals and gods alike we must die."

The collar of Seker-kha-bau, doubly priest of Anubis, thus takes on a sinister significance. The jackal figure and the six *ankh*-signs combine to show that the collar refers to the six-year period of Menkaure, and the combination can only be explained by the scene of Anubis and Ne-user-re. The " Great Name " of Seker-kha-bau shows also the priest's connection with the dead through the local Memphite god of the other world.

The question arises, if Seker-kha-bau were the summoner was he also the executioner, for I have already pointed out that the royal victim must be sacrificed, not murdered ; and the sacrifice must always be performed by a priest. So little is known of the early religion of Egypt that it is quite uncertain, though not unlikely, that the summoner and the sacrificial priest were one and the same. If this is so, the titles of the priests of Anubis assume a meaning and significance which reveal the primitive religion of Egypt in an unexpected aspect.

If, as Erman has pointed out, the name Osiris means simply the Occupier of the Throne, the inclusion of the Death-god in the Osirian Cycle is logical, for one of the central doctrines of the Osirian faith was the death, by violence, of the god. Seth's rôle of executioner is also in accordance with the modern Shilluk custom, for Seth was full brother to Osiris and was therefore the obvious candidate for the office. In primitive societies the King-killer was probably the successor to the throne, and in the legend Seth was aiming at the crown. Seker-kha-bau has among his priestly offices a title which is unexplained, but which refers to Seth.

I suggest then that in Seker-kha-bau must be seen the priest of Anubis who, masked as Anubis, announced to the king that the day of death was fixed and that also, as the official representative of Seth, he consummated the sacrifice.

6. Though Anubis has several epithets, I propose to discuss only three of them here.

(*a*)  *imj Wt*. This epithet has been variously explained, but to my mind the explanations leave much to be desired. The rare epithet  *Wtj* " He of Ut " (see p. 11 ; also GARSTANG, *Mahasna*, pl. viii, 1) should be considered in this connection. The determinative is usually called the city-sign, and therefore a " city of Ut " has been invented. *Wt* has also been called the " city of bandaging ", though it must be fairly obvious that no such city ever existed. The so-called " city-sign " originally denoted an enclosed space, which may have been inhabited or merely cultivated, hence its use in the names of farms and fields. It was not a town with streets and houses in our sense of the word ; it was not necessarily even a village or a hamlet. But the word *Wt* is well-known as the term for an oasis ; hence the epithet can be translated " He who is in " (or " from ") " the Oasis ".

(*b*) 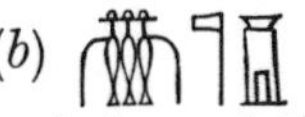 *ḫnti sḥ nṯr* " He who is in front of the shrine of the God ". In this title the shrine is always represented from the front, and in detailed examples the door is shown. It is a lattice-work shrine, and the meaning must be studied in connection with another latticed shrine of Anubis. Late representations of Anubis show a jackal couchant above a low flat structure which looks like an altar. The early form of this building is seen on the sealings from the Royal Tombs of Abydos, where the roof is made of lattice-work, like the walls, and is in the form of a jackal (see p. 9, fig. 1). If Anubis is regarded as connected with the Pharaoh only, this shrine must have a special royal significance. Modern Africa still practises certain customs which occasionally throw light on ancient religious rites, and this is a case in point. Among the Shilluk of the Upper Nile Valley the method of killing the king was to enclose him in an air-tight hut, specially built for the purpose, and let him die slowly of suffocation. After some months the death-hut was " broken down by the *ororo*, a grave was dug and the bones of the king were placed in it wrapped in the skin of one of the sacrificed oxen. A hut was built over the grave, and one or two others put up within the enclosure for the attendants on the new shrine, which had thus arisen " (SELIGMAN, *Pagan Tribes of the Nilotic Sudan*, pp. 91, 92). The hut-shrine, with the figure of the death-god cunningly woven into the actual structure, shows very clearly that it was a death-hut, and suggests that the royal victim was put to death, like the Shilluk King, in a special building. The euphemism for the King's death, " The two great Doors are shut," may refer to that early time and the closing of the doors of the death-hut. If the early Kings were put to death by the same method as the Shilluk chieftains and if, as I have suggested, the priest of Anubis was the royal executioner who closed the doors, the epithet " He who is in front of the shrine of the God " becomes intelligible, especially when it is remembered that in that title the shrine is always represented with the door visible. My contention, that the King and the God were one and the same as late as the Old Kingdom, receives confirmation in the tomb of Persen (MAR, *Mastabas*, pp. 299–301), where the formula for the dead man implores that he may " walk on the beautiful roads on which the worthy ones walk to *the King* ".

(*c*)  *nb t' ḏśr* ; var.  *ḫntï t' ḏśr*. This epithet again refers to Anubis as a death-god. In this connection the word *ḏśr* means " cleared, purified ", with the sense of driving away evil spirits or evil influences. The phrase *t' ḏśr* means a cemetery, and is used, according to Erman and Grapow (*Wtb.* v, 228), with special reference to Abydos, the royal burial-place of the Ist and IInd dynasties. This again brings Anubis into connection with royal deaths.

7. The combination of Horus and Anubis is again strong evidence that Anubis was in origin a purely royal deity. The falcon was the totem of the Pharaoh from the time of Narmer onwards. His four standards on the slate-palette are two falcons, a jackal, and the placenta or birth-sign. On the mace-head the standards are arranged in a different order, jackal, birth-sign, and the two falcons. If my interpretation is correct these four standards, which were the personal standards of the King, show his birth (the placenta), his death (the jackal), and his two totems (the falcons), one totem being for his career on earth, the other being the one into which he entered at death. The belief in the entry of the King into a falcon at death seems to be expressed in the words used to announce the death of Amenemhet I, " He has flown up to the horizon to join the Sun." And that the King had a falcon-totem for his lifetime is shown by the human-armed falcon on Narmer's slate palette, by innumerable instances of the falcon-names of Kings, and by the words applied to Senusert I, " The falcon has flown away." In the case of Narmer, I consider that the standards were carried two by two, the standards of birth and death having each its respective totem beside it.

CHAPTER II.

OTHER EARLY DEITIES.

8. BAST. The title of Zefau " Great One of *bst* " cannot refer to the goddess, whose name in the Old Kingdom (see MARIETTE, *Mastabas*, p. 70 ; PETRIE, *Medum*, pls. xvi, xx, xxi ; British Museum, No. 1324) is spelt  (abbreviated to  in later times). Bast was a cat-goddess, and the pot of perfume, which seems to be an integral part of her name, suggests either that the original animal was a civet cat or that the perfume was of that strong and rather acrid variety beloved of cats. The spelling out of the name appears to indicate that the early pronunciation was *śb't*, altered later by metathesis. The meaning would then be " She who causes to be a soul ", the " Soulifier ", if I may be permitted to coin a word. This name is parallel with the causative epithet applied to another deity  *ś-bk* " He who causes to be pregnant ".

Nothing is known of the ritual of Bast except the description by Herodotus (Book ii, 60) of the orgiastic ceremonies and dances held in her honour in the Delta. It is possible also that the perfume, with which she is so closely associated, had an intoxicating quality, and that her votaries like those of Bacchus felt themselves etherialized by the deity. This would explain the account given by Herodotus. The temple of Bubastis which so roused the enthusiasm of Herodotus, yielded on excavation no information as to her nature or rites ; but as the local deity she undoubtedly united in herself the powers of life and death, fertility and barrenness, within her own district.

In the fusion period Bast was identified with Sekhmet, who was a lioness, not a cat. When the theologians invented the marriages of gods, Sekhmet was paired off with Ptah, but Bast was always a deity without a consort. In the late period both goddesses were represented as enemies of snakes, but this is an attribute which should belong to Bast only. There is no record in Egypt, ancient or modern, of any kind of connection between lions and snakes ; on the other hand, in the country parts of modern Egypt cats are still regarded as snake-killers, and are often kept for that purpose. In the religion, which after all only reflected earthly ideas, the divine cat was the destroyer of evil symbolized as a snake.

The title " Great One of *bst* " is very rare, only two persons being recorded as the holders, Zefau and Ka-pu-Ra (MARIETTE, *Mastabas*, pp. 252, 275), both of Saqqara. The object which determines the word *bst* is the head of a lioness; this would seem to bring it into relation with the two feline goddesses, though the spelling with —•— shows that it is not identical with the name of Bast. The object appears to be a playing piece or chessman of the type which usually stands for the syllable *pḥ*. The title may belong to a civil office; the *Wörterbuch* gives only the vague term " Schatzbeamter " as the translation, but this is only because in the list of titles it precedes, or is written parallel with, the title *imj-r pr-ḥḏ*, which was the highest office in the Treasury. I suggest that the object represents a weight, probably of small size for weighing precious metals. Among ancient peoples the primary weights and measures were often regarded as sacred and were kept in the temple as the safest depository of the period, and there guarded by the priests. But in less troubled times the guardians might well be laymen. In the Vth dynasty conditions were settled, and it is quite possible that in Memphis, the capital of the country, a civilian guardian might be appointed; but the sanctity of the object would be indicated by the form, which placed it under the special protection of the lioness-goddess of the city.

9. HATHOR. The goddesses most frequently mentioned in the tombs of Saqqara are Hathor and Neith. Both were deities whose cult was widely spread, and lasted so long that their original aspect is almost lost; this is particularly the case in regard to Hathor. In late times she is fused with all other goddesses, especially with Isis as the Great Mother. But her position was comparatively humble in the Memphite nome, where she was identified with the Lady of the Sycomore. This title was entirely local in the Old Kingdom, though later it spread with her cult to other parts of Egypt. That she was worshipped elsewhere in the Old Kingdom under other titles is proved by her epithet at Dendera of " Lady of the Pillar " (MAR. *Mast.* p. 311 for name of pillar). As *Lady of the Sycomore* her priesthood at Memphis in the Old Kingdom consisted of women only; as *Lady of the Pillar* women were predominant in her service. There is only one record of a priesthood of hers as *Lady of Cusae*, and that is held by a man.

The explanation usually given of the name of the goddess is the literal translation of the hieroglyphs in which it is written, " House of Horus ". The attempt to prove that it means " Mother of the unborn Horus " is surely untenable. Had the Egyptians wished to call her the pregnant goddess, they would have done so openly and would not have taken refuge in a modest paraphrase. " Horus in the womb " (*Ḫnti-ḫt*) was a popular god at all times, particularly in the Middle Kingdom, and our modern ideas of propriety and modesty would not have affected the ancient Egyptian epithets for a goddess. The translation *House of Horus* means nothing as it stands, and should be abandoned and another translation sought.

BARTON (*Semitic and Hamitic Origins*, p. 168, ed. 1934) has attempted this when he suggests that the words are really *Ḥt-ḥrt*, translated as " She of the lofty House ". But here again the translation is inadmissible, as *ḥr* means " above, over ", not " lofty ". The Egyptian word for " lofty " is *ḳ'*.

There is, however, another possible explanation of the name Hathor, to which I would call attention. The T in the middle of the name is not explained by either of the derivations proposed. The Egyptian ⌓ survives into the Greek and Coptic transliterations only when it is a root-letter; when it is merely the feminine termination, as in the word *ḥt* (=), it disappears unless supported by a pronoun. The fact that the T remains shows that a pronoun was originally there; and that it could only have been the pronoun of the first person singular. This pronoun was often omitted in writing and probably in speaking, as well, but its presence would preserve the sound of the feminine termination. The first part of the name would then read " My house ". If the second part of the name means, as Barton has pointed out, some form of the adverb *ḥr* " above, over ", the name can be reasonably translated as " My house is above "; or as the feminised form *ḥrt* means " That which is above " and was commonly used as a term for the sky, i.e. the vault of heaven, the translation would then be " My house is the sky ", and would account, as nothing else does, for the identification of Hathor the cow with Nut the sky. The identification of Nut and Hathor has always been a puzzle, yet they were very closely connected. At Memphis Hathor is the Lady of the Sycomore, whose function was to provide the dead with food in the regions of the other world, but in later times it was Nut who had charge of the dead. Hathor was certainly a cow-goddess from the earliest period, for on the slate palette of Narmer she is represented, as she was represented throughout the whole course of Egyptian history, with a woman's face and cow's ears and horns. But the heavenly cow, who gives birth to the sun and moon, may be either Hathor or Nut indifferently. Even as late as Ptolemaic times the identification of Hathor and Nut is indicated by the figure of " Nut the Unknown " in the Hathor temple of Dendera.

In early times there seems to be no indication that Hathor was a Mother-goddess ; nor, until she was fused with Isis, had she a consort. She was not specifically connected with water or with agricultural fertility, that is to say with sowing and reaping, which may mean that she belongs to a pre-agricultural period, to the times of animal husbandry. She would thus be one of the primitive goddesses, and though her name may be Egyptian she could be fused with both native and foreign goddesses. Her identification with Ashtoreth-Karnaim, the cow-horned goddess of Babylonia, has been noted by MÜLLER, *Asien und Europa*, p. 313.

10. NEITH. Neith is another goddess who, in the Old Kingdom, was served by women only. Her cult was not so popular in Memphis and the South as that of Hathor, probably because she was essentially a goddess of the North. She had, however, an important shrine in Memphis. Her title, Neith, " North of the Wall," fixes its topographical position in relation to the shrine of Ptah, which was South of the Wall. This position was possibly arranged as being appropriate to a goddess of the North. Neith has two emblems, both of which were regarded as sufficiently sacred to be set on the sign of divinity (in the Ist dynasty they are set on a pole ; see PETRIE, *Royal Tombs* i, Front., ii, pl. x, 2). The emblems are : (*a*) crossed arrows, and (*b*) two bows in a case (*Ancient Egypt*, 1921, p. 36) ; these indicate that she was a goddess of the chase. The earliest examples of the emblems are from the royal tombs at Abydos and Naqada, and occur in the name of the queen, Neith-hotep. The meaning of the name is at present unknown ; it appears to be the same as that of the crown of Lower Egypt, which was itself a divinity.

11. RUI. The name  appears to be equivalent to the later 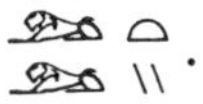. It is now well established by Erman, Sethe, and others that the duplication of a sign is not necessarily the duplication of the syllable in reading, but may represent the dual form. That being the case, the reading here would be *rwj* " The two lions ", not *rr* which is the word for a pig. The feminine form of this name is therefore not *rwrwtj* as written, but *rwtj* as Naville noted (*Sphinx*, 1902, p. 195). The meaning of the word has, I think, been discussed only by Naville (*op. cit.*), who, however, did not recognize the ⌓ as the feminine ending, but suggests that the *tj* is a *nisbe*-form, and that the word is an epithet of the sphinx.

If, though, the word is really a dual, the meaning may become clear in connection with the hitherto unexplained expression *rwtj wrtj*, which is said to refer to the great double gates of the palace or a temple. It has been inferred that the dual form of the word is due to the fact that the Egyptians used folding or double doors, and that therefore the word for door would naturally be in the dual. This seems hardly likely, for in the earliest example of the word for a door (on the slate palette of Narmer) the word is in the singular. It seems more probable that the word should be taken literally, and that *rwj* or *rwtj*—the two lions or two lionesses, in later times two sphinxes—were the images of animals who acted as guardians of the gate, one on each side of the entrance. A guardian of the door or gate is often a deity (cf. the god Janus), and it is therefore not surprising to find a priest of the cult.

One of the earliest examples of the lion or lioness as gate guardian is on a clay sealing of King Zer of the Ist dynasty from Abydos (Fig. 1). Some years ago Professor Petrie drew attention to the connection in this sealing between the shrine and the guardian lion with the triple bar on its back ; he took the bar to be the barrier in front of the shrine. A similar lion or lioness with a single bar on its back (Fig. 2) occurs on the wooden panel of Ra-hesy,

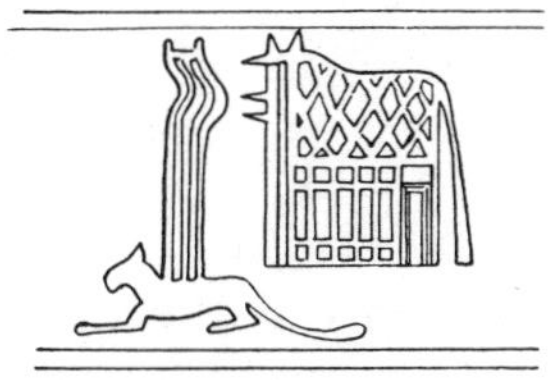

FIG. 1.

FIG. 2.

in the list of his titles. The inscription of Kay-em-hest gives the reading *rwj*, a masculine dual form of which the feminine would be *rwtj*. The early examples show what appears to be a maneless lion, hence the masculine word *rwj* ; the want of a mane suggested to the later Egyptians that the animal was female, and the feminine form *rwtj* was adopted.

An important point in regard to the lion-guardian is the form of the shrine on the clay sealing. It must have been made of lattice-work, and the upper part represents the jackal god, Anubis ; the ears, snout, and paws are over the front, the body of the animal extends over the whole edifice, and the tail hangs down to the ground at the back of the shrine. There are three examples of this shrine from Abydos, all of the same period (*Royal Tombs*, ii, pl. xvi, 114, 116, 117) ; only one shows the entire building, the others are incomplete but the characteristic tail is quite clear. This is a totally different type of shrine from those of the same early period represented on the slate palettes, mace-heads, sealings, and ebony tablets. It is obviously a special building connected with the god of death and presumably with the King in his aspect as a god. The form of the shrine, as shown on the sealing, may explain the reference to Anubis in the *Book of the Dead* (ch. lxxviii, 26), " He who is high on his *db'*," a word which is rendered " tomb " or " edifice ", or else left untranslated. I have given above (p. 6) my view as to the use and meaning of the death hut.

The name of Ruti occurs three times in the Pyramid Texts, the meaning in each instance being obscure. " Thy ennead is thine, O Atum and Ruti. Those who make their two gods and their two bodies are Shu and Tefnut " (W. 447). " Verily, the ka of this N. rises to the god, and brings him to Ruti and . . . him to Atum " (N. 2081). " Great is the honour of N. in the house of Ruti. Is expelled the fault belonging to N. by the expeller of evil in the presence of Khenti-irti in Letopolis " (N. 2086).

In the *Book of the Dead* the references are more frequent, but it must be remembered that in the New Kingdom much of the religion, which originally belonged to the Pharaoh alone, had become democratized and was used by lesser folk. The papyri of the XVIIIth dynasty (Nu and Nebseni) show a connection between Ruti and the idea of life after death. " O Atum, coming forth as the Great One of the waves, glorious like Ruti, make for him commands to the crew of Ra in the evening that the Osiris NN may live after death like Ra every day " (ch. xxxviii, B. 2). " I go in, I go out, my throat is not slit. I go down to the Boat of Maat. I mount (?) up to the Manzet-boat in the retinue of Ra at his side in his horizon. I live after I am dead every day. I am strong (*wśr*) like Ruti, for I live after I am dead " (ch. xxxviii, A. 7).

Ruti is also connected with the *nemes*-cloth, the striped head-dress of the Pharaoh. The root meaning of the word *nms* is not known, therefore the exact explanation of the word in the masculine form as applied to the royal head-cloth, or in the feminine form (*nmst*) as applied to a vase, is still to seek. There appears to be a connection between the nemset-vase and the cobra which suggests an original connection of the vase as well as the cloth with the King.

The references in the *Book of the Dead* are as follows : " Says Ruti, who is chief of the guardians of the House of the Nemes-cloth, who is in his cavern, Why dost thou turn back to the limits of heaven ? Behold, thou art noble (*s'ḥ*) in thy existences of Horus. The *nemes* is not against thee " (ch. lxxviii, 21). " Horus repeats to me that which his father Osiris said to him in the season and days of burial, when thou gavest to me the *nemes*-cloth. Says Ruti to me, Thou goest and comest upon the road of heaven, those who are in the ends of the horizon see thee. . . . Verily, he who is high on his shrine has bound for me the *nemes*-cloth at the command of Ruti. . . . I am high on my shrine, Ruti has bound the *nemes*-cloth on me (ch. lxxviii, 21, 3, 26).

The Negative Confession shows that Ruti was not a local deity, for he " comes forth from heaven " and not from a specified city. This also suggests that he belonged originally to the cycle of royal gods and not to a single town or to the people.

12. SESHAT (also transliterated as Sefekht-abui). Sethe (p. 11) calls this deity the Goddess of Architecture. At the early period to which Seker-kha-bau belonged, architecture in the present sense of the word was still in its infancy. It would be better to call her the Goddess of Building, as this epithet would cover all types of building from the most primitive reed-hut to the most stately stone temple. The hieroglyphs on the false-door of Seker-kha-bau show that at that period so great and important a god as Seth had only a lattice-and-thatch shrine for his worship ; temples copied in stone from reed and wood prototypes were only just beginning. Seshat must therefore be the deity of hut-building, and this is, I think, shown by the hieroglyph of her name (see *Saq. Mast.* I, PL. XXXIX,

51). The central pillar is of reeds firmly lashed together and ending in the well-known *kheker*-ornament. On this central pillar are laid three cross-beams, also made of lashed papyrus reeds, which span the hut from side to side; the combination of beams and pillar give the effect of an open flower owing to the peculiar method used by the Egyptian artist of representing a building partly in plan and partly in elevation. A domed roof of thatch rests on the ends of the beams and on the top of the central pillar. This is then the aspect of a hut before the lattice side-screens are put in position; it represents the essential parts of the building, the screens being non-essential. The ornament at the top may be the feathers of divinity, but are more probably the representation in highly stylized form of the bunches of straw with which the topmost layer of thatch is finished. Huts of this type are to be found in Africa at the present time.

Seshat is also known as the Goddess of Writing, but she was rather the Recorder of the years of the King's reign than the deity of actual writing. If, as I have tried to prove, Seker-kha-bau was the herald of death to the King and perhaps the sacrificial priest of the divine victim, he might very well include in his duties the recording of the events of that victim's reign. In the temple of Karnak the goddess is called "Seshat of Pe-Dep"; remembeing that the death-oracle came to Menkaure from Buto (Pe-Dep), there is here another connection linking Seker-kha-bau, by his priesthood of the goddess, with the ritual death of the King.

CHAPTER III.

TRANSLATIONS AND INSCRIPTIONS IN SAQQARA MASTABAS I.

By Kurt Sethe.

[Titles of office were not tabulated and studied all together until 1926, twenty-one years after these chapters were written. From this study, consistent equivalents of hieroglyphs and translation have been worked out and indexed in *Ancient Egypt*, 1924–7. These values have been added here in square brackets.—F. P.]

13. TOMB OF KHA-BAU-SEKER. PLS. I, II.

Name. read *ḫ'j-b'w-Skr* "The glory of Seker shines". Analogous names are *ḫ'j-b'w-Ptḥ* "The glory of Ptah shines", *ḫ'j-k'w-R'* "The spirits of Ra shine", *ḫ'j-nfrw-R'* "The beauties of Ra shine". The *little name* is the name of an animal *ḥtś*, which is regarded by Miss Murray, judging by the determinative, as a mongoose. The technical term for the "little name" of a person is not *rn šr*, but appears (by the variant here given) to be *rn nḏś*.

Titles.

1. *ḫrp rwt šm' mḥw* "[Controller of the borderers] of the South and North".

2. (var.) *ḫrp ''wt* "[Controller of the brewing] women".

3. (var.) *ḫrp 'bwt* "[Controller of the washing] women".

4. (var. without , var. without) "[Controller of the hoe and knife flaking" (lit.: loosening)].

5. *ḫrp ḥmjt išt* "[Controller of the registered] workmen".

6. (var.) *rḫ nfrt ḥr ib nb-f* "Knowing what is pleasant for the heart of his lord".

7. (var.) *irï ḫ nï-śwt* "[Courtier]".

8. *s' 'b* (?) "[Guard of the cattle]".

9. *ḥm-nṯr Sš't* "Prophet of the goddess of architecture".

10. (var.) see *Aeg. Inschr. von Berlin*, i, t. 31; GARSTANG, *Mahasna*, pl. viii, 2.

11. (var. var.).

12. *ḥm-nṯr* . . . "Prophet of . . ."

13. (var. var.) *ḥk' n nṯr*.

14. (var.) *sḫnw pr-wr Śtḥ* ". . . of the temple of Seth".

Date, IIIrd dynasty.

Family. Wife *irï ḫ nï-śwt Nfr-ḥtp-Ḥtḥr* "The [courtier], Beautiful is the peace of Hathor". Her "little name" is Tepes.

Stele of the man, Pl. I.

The lower part of the stele is occupied by a long list of offerings, which differs completely from the usual lists of the IVth–VIth dynasties. Note the determinatives which occur under the name of each object, and the generic title which stands above the several groups.

In the centre under the panel are the names of woven fabrics. These are divided into three kinds, *ïdmj* "Red stuff", "*sḫr*-fabric" and "‘’-fabric". Then follow lists of various vessels and household gear. To right and left are identical lists of beer, wines, fruits, and grain.

Pl. II. On the architrave are the name and some of the titles of Kha-bau-Seker (see p. 11).

On the stele of Nefer-hotep-Hathor the list of offerings is shorter than on that of her husband, but gives several variants. Of these the most interesting is, that whereas on the stele of the man various vessels are represented under the headings and, here they all appear under the one heading *śḫpt*.

14. Tomb of Ka-em-Hesut. Pl. III, 1.

Name. *K'-m-ḥswt* "The ka is in favour". Compare the analogous names , , , , .

Titles.

1. *s'-mr-f* A priestly title which is also known as an epithet of Horus.

2. (reading doubtful) "Sculptor".

3. *ïmy prwy* "He who is in the two Houses". An engineer's title borne by the High Priest of Memphis as "the great Leader of the artisans", and also by the "chief of all the [carpentry and brickwork] of the King".

4. ?

5. *ḥm-nṯr rwrw* (?) *ḫntj ḥt-nṯr* "Prophet of the Lion-god who is in front of the House of natron" (For a further discussion of this god see pp. 9, 10.)

6. *ḥnk nï-śwt ïm'ḫw-f* "The Friend of the King, honoured by him". *Hnk nï-śwt* is also a special title of the High Priests of Memphis.

15. Lintel from the tomb of Khuyu-en-Ptah. Pl. III, 3.

Name. *ḫwjw-n-Ptḥ* "He whom Ptah has protected". Compare the analogous names *Ś-'nḫw-n-Ptḥ*, *Ïrjw-n-'ḫ'j*, and the name of a later King *Śḳnjw-n-R'*.

Titles.

1. *imj-r ḥmtjw* "[Intendant] of the Artisans".

2. *ḥm-nṯr Ptḥ* "Prophet of Ptah".

3. *ḥm-nṯr Skr* "Prophet of Seker".

The same person occurs in an inscription in the Wadi Hammamat of the time of Pepy I (see L. *D.* ii, 115 *b*).

16. Alabaster Table of Offerings of Hotep-Akhti-Her. Pl. III, 4.

Name. *Ḥtp-'ḫtj-ḥrj* A name which contains the word *'ḫtj*, an epithet of the sun-god, which in later times is found only with the name . Compare *'ḫtj-ḥtp*, *‘’j-'ḫtj*, *irjw-n-'ḫtj*, *n-św-'ḫtj*. The form with *ḥtp* and *ḥr*, which occurs in the name is very ancient and is found even in the 1st dynasty (*Royal Tombs*, ii, pl. xxvi, 70).

Titles.

1. *s'b irj-Nḫn* "Judge belonging to Hierakonpolis".

2. *ḥm-nṯr M'ʿt* " Prophet of the goddess of Truth ".

Date. A man of the same name and with the same titles lived under and of the Vth dynasty (see MARIETTE, *Mastabas*, p. 340).

In the inscription the formula should read

17. TOMB OF THE SHEIKH EL BELED. PL. III, 5.

Name. *K'-ʿpr.* A common name in the Old Kingdom.

Title. *ḥrj-ḥb ḥrj-ḏ'ḏ'.* " Chief lector-priest."

The inscription is on the lintel of the great granite false-door.

18. TOMB OF PTAH-HOTEP I. PLS. IV, V.

Son and successor of Ptah-hotep desher.

Titles.

1.
2.
3.
4.

for these, see Sect. 19.

5. (without on architrave) *imj-r iswj ḫkr ni-śwt* " [Intendant of the registers] of the two store-houses of the King's [favourite] ".

6. see sect. 19, 20.

7. " [Intendant] of the *usekht*-hall ".

8. " [Intendant] of the two granaries ".

9. " [Intendant] of the Treasury ".

10. " [Intendant] of the six Great Houses " (higher courts of Justice).

11. " [Intendant of the registers] of that which is under seal ".

12. *imj-r iswj mrt* " [Intendant of the register] of the two houses of the slaves ".

13. See Sect. 14.

19. TOMB OF PTAH-HOTEP DESHER. PL. VI.

Name. *Ptḥ-ḥtp dšr* Ptah-hotep the Red. For other colour designations, compare *Ś'bw km* Sabu the Black.

Titles.

1.

2. " [Leader] ".

3. " High-Court judge, Vezir ".

4. " [Intendant] of the scribes of the [royal documents] ".

5. " [Intendant] of all the works of the King ".

6. " [Intendant of registers of the Double House of the royal Favourites]."

7. " [Intendant of the Court of Six] ".

8. " [Intendant of registers] of the Double House of things under seal ".

9. " [Controller] of the *usekht*-hall ".

Date. First half of the Vth dynasty.

On the architrave above the doorway of the outer chamber is an inscription in two lines, containing a formula for the dead and the titles and name of the deceased : " May the King be gracious and grant, may Anubis be gracious, he who is in front of the Divine Hall, he who is in Ut, the lord of Ta-zoser, he who is on the Hill of the Slug, he who is in front of Sepa (Hipponon), that he may be buried in the necropolis in the western desert, at a very good old age, as one honoured by the great God," (here follow the titles) " Ptah-hotep the Red ".

On the drum of the door is the name of the deceased, preceded by his principal title : " [High Court] judge and Vezir."

CHAPTER IV.

By Kurt Sethe.

20. TOMB OF PTAH-HOTEP II. PLS. VIII–XVII.

Titles.

(*a*) General titles.

1. *ỉrj-p't.*

2. *ḥ'tj-'* [Leader].

3. *ỉrj P* "Belonging to Buto".

4. *śḏ'tj* (?) *bỉtj* "[Royal sealer]".

5. *śmr w'tj n mrwt* "[Companion peer beloved]".

6. *mdw rḫjt* "[Spokesman of the *rekhyut*]".

7. *ḫrp wśḫt* "[Controller] of the palace".

8. *inkmt.*

9. (var. with) *ḥrj śšt' n nỉ-śwt* "[Over the secrets] of the King".

10. *ḥrj-śšt' n wḏt-mdw nt nỉ-śwt* "[Over the secrets] of all commands of the King".

(*b*) Juridical and administrative service.

11. *s'b t'jtj ṯ'* "[High Court] judge and Vezir".

12. *ỉmj-r k't nbt nt nỉ-śwt* "[Intendant] of all the works of the King".

13. *ỉmj-r sš ' nỉ-śwt* "[Intendant] of the scribes of the archives of the King".

(*c*) Treasury service.

14. *ỉmj-r ỉḫt nbt nt nỉ-śwt* "[Intendant] of all the things of the King".

15. *ỉmj-r šnwtj* "[Intendant] of the two granaries".

16. *ỉmj-r prwj ḥḏwj* "[Intendant] of the two White Houses," i. e. the finance department.

17. *ỉmj-r iswj ḫrjt śd't* [Intendant of the registers of the] two Storehouses of what is under seal. Cf. MARIETTE, *Mastabas*, p. 230.

18. *ỉmj-r w'bt* "[Intendant of the pure place = tomb]".

19. *ỉmj-r prwj nbw* "[Intendant] of the two Houses of Gold".

20. *ỉmj-r ḫkr nỉ-śwt* "[Intendant] of the royal favourites".

21. (also without) *ḫrj-ḥb ḥrj-ḏ'ḏ' sš dmḏt* "Chief lector-priest, scribe of the divine books".

Family. *s'-f śmśw mrjj-f tpj ḥr nỉ-śwt 'ḫtj-ḥtp* "His eldest son, who is loved by him, the First under the King, Akhety-hotep". For the reading of the name, see p. 12. Probably the same as the Chief judge and Vezir whose tomb was published by Davies (*The Mastaba of Ptahhetep and Akhethetep*) and whose son, Ptah-hotep, was the overseer of the chief city under Asesa.

Inscriptions.

PL. VIII, West wall.

Titles and name of the deceased.

Formulae :

On the left : (*a*) . . . "that he may be buried in the necropolis in the western desert, at a very good old age, as one honoured by the great God", (the titles), "Ptah-hotep"; (*b*) . . . "that offerings shall be presented to him on New Year's Day (the first of Thoth), on the festival of Thoth (18th of Thoth), on the first day of the year (1st of Tybi), at the Uag-festival, on the great festival of Seker, at the rising of Min, on the *saz*-festival, for Ptah-hotep".

On the right : (*a*) Like the left ; (*b*) ". . . that he may go upon the beautiful roads upon which the honoured ones go, in peace, in peace, to every great God."

PL. XI. East Wall. The registers are counted from below and begin on the left.

Fourth register (from the bottom). A donkey about to be loaded is being dragged to the heap of sheaves, above which is *pḥt*.

Third register, beginning on the left. (*a*) The sheaves are being thrown on a stack *wbś*, (*b*) The corn is being trodden out by donkeys on the threshing floor. The discourse of the drivers *ỉ' ḥ' m'-k ỉrt-k, ỉrmj ḥ'-k ỉm-śn*, is not comprehensible, though it always occurs with some variations in this scene. (*c*) The threshed corn is heaped up in piles with forks *ỉʿbw* "Sweeping together"; cf. MARIETTE, *Mastabas*, pp. 181, 289. cf. (L. *D.* ii, 4), and the of the inscription of Una. (*d*) Women separating the corn from the chaff by winnowing. *ḫʿḫʿ ỉt ỉn dwt* "Winnowing the barley by slaves". Also *ỉhj ỉt.*

Second register. (*a*) Bird-catching. Men closing a clap-net on the birds. *šḫt 'pdw ỉn wḥʿw nw pr-ḏt* "The catching of birds in a net by the bird-catchers of the endowed property". Above, the man who is giving the signal to close the net: *rdjt šḫt* "Causing the catching in the net". (*b*) The captured birds are being carried to the deceased (whose figure is now broken away). The first two men who are thus engaged are called Snezem-yb and Ptah-hotep.

First register (the lowest). Scenes of slaughtering. (*a*) Man in the dress of the upper classes, *wʿb Šḫmt šḥḏ snw Wnn-nfr* "Priest of Sekhmet and [expert] physician, Unen-nefru". He attends the slaughtering to ensure the "purity" of the animals (see DAVIES, *Ptah-hetep*). The same person is mentioned in the tomb of Akhethetep (DAVIES, op. cit., ii, pl. xviii). For physicians as priests of the goddess Sekhmet, see ERMAN, *Aegypten*, p. 467, 1st ed. (*b*) A man whets a knife. *pḏt dś ỉn śšmw* "Sharpening the knife by the butcher". Another, who is about to cut off the hind-leg of the ox, says to his comrade who holds the leg, *nḏr nw ḥn-k m ʿnḫ* "Hold this as tight as you can". "I am doing so," is the reply. (*c*) An ox is being eviscerated. *šdt ḥ'tj ỉn śšmw* "The taking out of the heart by the butcher". (*d*) A man, who is cutting off a foreleg, says to the comrade who holds it, *ỉṯj ỉr-k mnḫj śšmw pw* "Pull well, you butcher". The answer is *ỉrj-j r ḥst-k wrt* "I am doing (it) so that thou shalt greatly praise" (see below). (*e*) A man whetting a knife *pḏt dś* "The sharpening of a knife". The foreleg has been cut off from the ox, *štp ỉw'* "The dismemberment of the ox". (*f*) The same. The man who cuts says, *ỉṯj ỉr-k mnḫj ḥn-k mʿnḫ ntj ḥnʿ* "Pull as hard as thou canst, my comrade". The other man, who holds the leg, answers, *ỉrj-j r ḥst-k* "I do (it) so that thou shalt praise". (*g*) Two men cutting up an ox from which the legs have already been removed. One says, *sfṯ r nfr ntj ḥnʿ* "Cut well, my comrade". The other replies, *mk ỉrj-j r ḥst-k* "See, I am doing (it) so that thou shalt praise".

PLS. IX, X. South Wall.

Lower register. The villages in Upper Egypt belonging to the deceased, typified by women, bring their produce to their lord. *ỉnt nḏt-ḥr ỉn nwt nt pr-ḏt nt šmʿw* "The bringing of the tribute by the villages of the endowed property in Upper Egypt". The villages are named, some after the kings who had bestowed them on the deceased or his ancestors, some after the deceased himself.

(1) *Mrj Rʿ ʿnḫ Ỉssj* "Reʿ desires that Asesa shall live".

(2) *Nfr-ḫʿw Ỉ-k'w-Ḥr* "Beautiful is the appearing of Y-kau-Hor".

(3) *Mrj Ḥr ʿnḫ Wśr-k'-f* " Horus desires that User-kaf shall live ".

(4) *Mrj Nḫbjt ʿnḫ K'k'j* " Eileithyia desires that Kakay shall live ".

(5) *Nfr ḥswt Ỉk'w-Ḥr* " Beautiful is the praise of Ykau-Hor ". This place is situated in the nome of Herakleopolis (see Davies, *Ptahhetep*, ii, pl. x).

(6) *Śnṯr Ptḥḥtp* " Incense of Ptah-hotep ".

(7) *Śḫt Ptḥḥtp* " *Sekhet*-corn of Ptah-hotep ".

(8) *Rpt* (?) *Ptḥḥtp* " Chapel of Ptah-hotep ".

(9) *Ỉ'gt Ptḥḥtp* " . . . of Ptah-hotep ". According to Dümichen (*Res.*, ii, 5) is not a variant of as one might suppose. See also L. *D.* ii, 80*b*, and Dümichen, *Res.*, i, 2.

(10) *Mnʿt Ptḥḥtp* " Wet-nurse of Ptah-hotep ".

(11) *Ḥtpt Ptḥḥtp* " Food offerings of Ptah-hotep ".

(12) *Ỉst Ptḥḥtp* " Boundary-house of Ptah-hotep ".

(13) *Śnb Ptḥḥtp* " Health of Ptah-hotep ".

(14) *ʿnḫ Ptḥḥtp* " Life of Ptah-hotep ".

(15) *P't Ptḥḥtp* " Offering of Ptah-hotep ".

(16) *mns' Ptḥḥtp* " Libation-vase of Ptah-hotep ".

(17) *Śmnt Ptḥḥtp* " . . . of Ptah-hotep " (see Dümichen, *Res.*, i, 2; ii, 5).

The deceased receives the procession. *m'' in* (here follow the titles) *Ptḥḥtp* " Seeing by " (titles) " Ptah-hotep ". In front of him his eldest son is handing him a list of gifts *rdjt sš n nḏt-ḥr* " Delivering the writing of the tribute ".

Upper register. Remains of a procession of men bringing gifts to a large seated figure of the deceased. The names which are preserved are :—

(1) *'ḫtj-ḥtp* Akhety-hotep. Probably the eldest son of the deceased.

(2) *Rwḏ.*

(3) *K'j-ḥp.*

(4) *Ỉrj-iś.*

(5) *N-ʿnḫ Mn.*

(6) *Śšmw.*

(7) *Nfr-śšmw-f.*

(8) *K'j-ḥp.*

(9) . . . *Śšmw* . . .

(10) . . . . . .

(11) *Śpśś-Ptḥ.*

A detached fragment of this procession (a man carrying dates) is on Pl. XVII, 6.

Pl. XII. North Wall. The representations correspond exactly with those of the South Wall.

In the lower register the villages of Lower Egypt are figured. The remains of the title of the scene : . . . . . . *nt pr-ḏt nt mḥw* " (The bringing of the tribute of the villages) of the endowed property in Lower Egypt ", and the name of the first village *Ś-ʿnḫ Ḥr Ỉssj* " Horus makes Asesa to live ", are on a detached fragment, Pl. XVII, 7. The same village occurs in the tomb of Akhethetep (Davies, *Ptahhetep*, ii, pls. x, xii), where it is stated to be in the province of Lower Egypt. Of the others the following names remain :—

(1) *Mrj M''t Ỉssj* " Truth loves Asesa ". The same place is mentioned in the tomb of his son Akhet-hotep as belonging to the " Right side of the Harpoon nome " (Davies, op. cit., ii, pl. x), and in the tomb of his other son, Ptah-hotep, to the Harpoon nome (Dümichen, *Res.*, ii, 15).

(2) *Ḏb't Wśr-k'-f* (see Mariette, *Mastabas*, p. 196; Dümichen, op. cit., ii, 15). Mentioned in the tomb of his son as being in the (Davies, op. cit., ii, pls. x, xiii, xv).

(3) *Mrj Śpdw K'k'j* " The god Sopdu (of the Arabian nome) loves Kakay ".

(4) *Śḥd Ḏd-f-Rʿ* " Dad-ef-Reʿ is heavenly ".

(5) *Nfr wḏt Ś'ḥw-Rʿ* " What Sahu-Re commands is good ".

(6) *Nbś Ptḥḥtp* " *Nebes*-fruit of Ptah-hotep ".

(7) *Ỉ't Ptḥḥtp* " Place of Ptah-hotep ".

(8) *Ḥbnnt Ptḥḥtp* " *Hebnent*-food of Ptah-hotep ".

(9) *Grgt Ptḥḥtp* " Establishment of Ptah-hotep ".

(10) *Ỉšd Ptḥḥtp* " *Ashed*-berries of Ptah-hotep ".

(11) . . . *Ptḥḥtp* " Handmaiden of Ptah-hotep " (see Mariette, *Mastabas*, p. 398).

(12) *Ỉnt Ptḥḥtp* " Valley (?) of Ptah-hotep ".

(13) *Ỉrt Ptḥḥtp* " Work of Ptah-hotep ".

Upper register. On the left the deceased was represented seated before a heap of offerings, the end of which *ḫ't wdḥw* "The best of the table", and *śtpwt* "Limbs of oxen and geese", still remain. Fragments of the list with the words *dżw-śḫr* "Beer", and *t' imj t'* "Country bread" are on PL. XVII, 8, 10.

A row of men bearing gifts: "Bringing the offerings for the dead by the [expert] deputy-superintendent of the funeral priests, the scribes of the [guard] and funeral priests of the endowed property," etc. The names of the persons are as follows:—

(1) The eldest son of the deceased, Akhety-hotep.

(2) . . . *s'b 'ḏ mr śḥḏ ḥm-k' Nw-ḥk'w* "Judge and [conservator of canals, expert servant] of the dead, Nu-hekau".

(3) . . . *śḥḏ ḥm-k'* . . .

(4) *s'b śḥḏ sš śḥḏ ḥm-k' Ittj* "Judge and [expert] scribe, [expert servant] of the dead, Ateta".

(5) *s'b sš śḥḏ ḥm-k' Ptḥḥtp* "Judge, scribe, [expert servant] of the dead, Ptah-hotep".

(6) *sš s' 'ḫtjḥtp* "Scribe of the [guard], Akhety-hotep".

(7) *sš s' s'b sš Ḳdnś* "Scribe of the [guard], judge and scribe, Qednes".

(8) *m śr Ij-ḏf'* "... I-zefa".

(9) *sš pr 'ḳt n njwtiïw* "The scribe of that which comes in for the inhabitants of the town".

PLATE XIV, 2. Offerings being brought to the tomb. Of the inscriptions very little remains. On the left at the top is the name ; on the left below, are the name "Ka-hap" and the title *śmśw wḫrt* "The elder of the [watch-house]".

PL. XVII. *Altar.* Titles and name of the deceased.

Fragments. Nos. 7, 8, 10 belong to the North Wall (see above).

No. 5 is from the South Wall (see above). No. 4 gives the name of a *śmr w'tj Nḏm-'nḫ* "[Companion-peer], Nezem-ankh".

21. TOMB OF ATETA. PLS. XVIII, XIX.

Name. *Ittj rn-f ''j 'nḫ-irj-iś* "Ateta, his great name Ankh-yry-ys".

Titles.

(1) *śmśw ist* ["Elder of the registers"], see 16 in next list.

(2) *imj prwj* "[He who is in the Double House]".

(3) *imj-r 'ḥ'* "[Intendant] of the palace".

(4) *wr mḏ šm'w* "[Mayor of the Southern Ten council]".

(5) *imj-r wḏ-mdw n wśḫt* "[Intendant of the dividing words] of the Court of Justice" (or "of the palace").

(6) *ḫrp mrwj ni-śwt* "[Controller of the royal canals]".

(7) *ḫrp tm'* "[Controller of the archers]". See L. *D.* ii, 101*a*, and PETRIE, *Medum*, pl. ix.

(8) *imj-r k't nbt nt ni-śwt* "[Intendant] of all the works of the King".

(9) *imj-r mst-t.* The word *mst-t* "[Child-porters]" appears here for the first time in its correct form. Otherwise it is spelt , the *m* being placed after the *ś* (see LACAU, *Rec. des Trav.*, and SETHE, *Verbum*, i, 277).

(10) *im'ḫw ḫr nṯr ''j* "Honoured by the great God".

(11) *im'ḫw ḫr ni-śwt r'nb* "Honoured by the King every day".

PLS. XVIII, XIX.

Panel. The deceased is seated before a table of offerings, by the side of which is a short formula wishing every possible good thing.

Architrave. The usual formula *ḥtp dj ni-śwt,*

desiring for the deceased a good burial and also funeral offerings on all feast days.

Drum. Name of the deceased with the most important titles.

Side columns. On the left the titles of the deceased. On the right a *ḥtp dj ni-św.t* formula: "May Anubis, who is in Ut, grant that he may go upon the beautiful roads every day to the Field of Offerings, to the places . . . as an honoured one, the (titles), Ateta."

CHAPTER V.

By Kurt Sethe.

22. Tomb of User-Neter. Pls. XX–XXV.

Name. Read *Wśr-nṯr* "The God is mighty", a form like *Wśr-k'-f* "His ka is mighty" (Οὐσερχερής). In writing, the word "God" is put first in the customary manner. The use of the generic word *nṯr* "God" in place of the name of a special god must not be taken as a sign of a monotheistic conception; what is meant is the god of the city in which dwelt the person so named.

On the drum of the outer door he is called "The old" to distinguish him from a younger member of the family with the same name, perhaps a grandson.

Titles.

(1) *tpj ḫr ni-św.t* "First under the King". This must be the principal title of the deceased, as it begins every column of titles and is the only one mentioned on the drums of the doors.

(2) *mdw rḫjt* "[Spokesman of the *rekhyut*]".

(3) *imj-r sš ' ni-św.t* "[Intendant] of the scribes of the documents of the King".

(4) *imj-r wśḫt,* [Intendant] or

(5) *ḫrp wśḫt* "[Controller] of the Wide Hall" (the royal palace).

(6) *s'b 'nḏ mr* "Judge and [conservator of canals]".

(7) *wr mḏ šm'w* "Great one of the [council of] Ten of Upper Egypt".

(8) *śḥḏ wr(w) mḏ šm'w* "[Expert] of the [Mayors of the council] of Ten of Upper Egypt".

(9) *inkmt.*

(10) *nśt ḫntjt* (follows the titles *wr-mḏ* or *s'b 'nḏ mr*).

(11) *imj-r k't nbt nt ni-św.t* "[Intendant] of all the works of the King".

(12) (var.) *ḥrj sšt' n wḏt-mdw nbt nt ni-św.t* "Over the secrets of all the commands of the King".

(13) var. *wḏ-mdw m'' n ḥrjw wḏbw* "Actual commander of the overseers of lands".

(14) *ḫrp sšw irj śpr* "[Controller of the scribes of petitions]".

(15) *ḫrp sšw nbw* "[Controller] of all scribes".

(16) *śmśw ist* "[Elder of the registers]". This title is held in the Pyramid Texts, T. 87 *passim*, by the servant of the god Ptah, who is regarded as the god of art and handicrafts.

(17) *ḥm-nṯr M''t* "Prophet of the goddess Maāt".

(18) *imj-r wrt* "[Intendant] of the Great House".

(19) "[Over the secrets of private decisions] of the Great House". The "Six Great Houses" is the term for the higher Courts of Justice of the country, the Court of Appeal, and others.

(20) *imj ib n nb-f* "The favourite of his lord".

(21) *ḥrj sšt' n mdw nṯr* "[Over the secrets] of the divine words", i.e. the ancient holy language of Egypt.

(22) *ḥrj wḏbw m ḥt-'nḫ* "Overseer of lands in the House of Life".

(23) *im'ḫw*

nṯrw nbw ḫrt-nṯr " Honoured by the gods, the lords of the necropolis ".

(24) *im'ḫw ḫr nṯr 'ʿj* " Honoured by the great God ".

Date. The middle of the Vth dynasty, as the eldest son appears to have been contemporary with Dad-ka-Ra.

Family.

1. Pl. XXIV (Niche). Wife. *śnt-ḏt ḥmt-f mrjt-f ḫkrt ni-śwt im'ḫwt ḫr ni-śwt Ḫnwt* " [Eternal sister], his wife, his beloved, the [favourite], of the King, honoured by the King, Khenut ". She therefore belonged to the King's harem. The expression is often found in the Old Kingdom, but the exact meaning is not known.

2. Pls. XXI, XXIII. Son. *s'-f śmśw mr-f śḥḏ wʿb im'ḫ ḫr it-f sš ʿ ni-śwt ḫft ḥr mrr nb-f Špśś-Rʿ.* " His eldest, his beloved son, the [expert] priest, honoured by his father, the scribe of the records before the face of the King, he whom his lord loves, Shepses-Ra." Probably the same man whose tomb Lepsius found at Saqqara (L. *D.*, ii, 60–4). He held under King Asesa (*Íssj*) the same offices as our User-neter; and his eldest son was likewise called User-neter.

3. Pls. XXI, XXIII. Son *s'-f mr-f im'ḫw ḫr it-f s'b sš Wśr-nṯr* " His son, beloved by him, he who is honoured by his father, the judge and scribe, User-neter ".

Description of the plates.

Pl. XX. Stele of the west wall. In the upper and outer pair of columns, the titles of the deceased are combined with the formula for the dead. Above: " May the King be gracious and grant, may Anubis be gracious, he who is before the Hall of the God, he who dwells in Ut, that he may be buried in the necropolis at a good old age " (titles) " User-neter ".

Right and left: " May Osiris be gracious and grant, he who is before Dedu " (Busiris in the Delta), " that he may go in peace upon the beautiful paths of the West, on which the honoured ones " (i.e. the blessed dead) " go to the great God, the Lord of the necropolis " (here follow the titles) " User-neter ". It is worth noting the omission of the King in this formula.

Pl. XXV. The drums of the two doors. As usual these mention only the name of the deceased with one of the principal titles, here *tpj ḫr ni-śwt*. On the drum of the outer door, which was naturally the last to be inscribed, he is called " the old ", to distinguish him from a younger person of the same name (see p. 18).

Architrave. The deceased seated; before him an inscription consisting of his titles and three wishes for him: (1) " That he may be buried in his grave in the West, at a good old age, by the great God.[1] (2) That funeral offerings may be brought to him on the Great Festival, the festival of the Heat, the rising of Min, and all other festivals through the length[2] of eternity. (3) That he may go on the beautiful roads of the West, on which the gods love to go, in peace to[3] the beautiful West, to the gods, the lords of the West."

On the walls of the doorway are very suitably placed the representations of the funeral priests bringing offerings for the dead into the tomb. Inscription: . . . *śḫpjt iḫt in ḥmw-k' wʿbjw* " The bringing of offerings by [the servants of the ka] who act *wʿb* " (for the deceased).

The deceased (with his titles inscribed above him) sits before a table of offerings. Above the table is a great list of offerings which are brought to him by numerous persons in five registers.

First register. (*a*) Two men kneeling, each presenting two vessels. *ḥkn in wtj* " The offering of liquids " (*ḥkn* written with an arm presenting a vessel) " by the Uty-priests ".

(*b*) A *ḫrj-ḥb* " Lector-priest ", recognisable by the band across his breast, holds a roll of papyrus, and with uplifted hand recites a text. *wdn iḫt rʿ-bn* " Offerings shall be made every day ", he says.

[1] Mariette, *Mastabas*, p. 95.

[2] The before is omitted

[3] The is omitted.

(*c*) Man bringing two strips of cloth *wnḫjw* " Two bandages ".

(*d*) Man offering incense. *k'p śnṯr* " The burning of incense ". The first sign is remarkable. The thurifers recur in each of the following registers, as it is the necessary form for the consecration of offerings. The inscription is always the same.

Second register. (*a*) Kneeling man pouring water on the ground. *s't* " Pouring on the ground ". Cf. No. 1 of the list of offerings. The word is a determinative of *s'ṯw* " Ground ", Coptic ⲉⲥⲏⲧ.

(*b*) Standing man pouring water from a pitcher. The inscription (probably *ḳbḥ*) is broken away.

(*c*) Man offering incense. Inscription as above.

(*d*) Three people without inscription.

Third register. (*a*) A *śḥḏ ḥmw-k'* " [Expert servant of the ka] " offers a goose.

Fourth register. (*a*) The eldest son of the deceased Shepses-Ra (see p. 19) offers a goose.

(*b*) The second son, User-neter, offers incense. Cf. Nos. 2 and 13 of the list of offerings.

(*c*) Man bringing two strips of linen. *wnḫjw*. Cf. No. 12 of the list.

(*d*) " [Servant of the ka] " pours water out of a jug " Libation of two drops ". Cf. No. 14 of the list.

(*e*) Man carrying a platter for food *ḥtpt nì-śwt* " Royal offering ". Cf. No. 16 of the list.

(*f*) Man carrying a little table with food *f't*. Cf. the and of the offering lists in the Pyramids and elsewhere.

(*g*) People with various gifts.

Fifth register. (*a*) Man offering a goose. No inscription.

(*b*) Incense bearer. Inscription as above.

(*c*) People with various gifts.

Below all these scenes runs a sixth register, in which the slaughter of oxen is shown. Beginning on the right :—

(*a*) A hornless animal is being bound *int rnt ìw't n ìḫt 'bdwt* " The bringing of a heifer for the monthly repast ".

(*b*) Three scenes of slaughtering, in each of which on the right is a butcher sharpening his flint knife by chipping *pḏt dś in śšmw* " Sharpening the knife by the butcher ". In the first scene the ox is eviscerated. *ìmj ḥ'tj* " Give me the heart ", says the impatient man on the left, who is already laden with the haunch and is waiting to carry the heart away. In the second scene a fore-leg, in the third a hind-leg, is being removed. *ìṯj ìr-k* " Take ", says the man, who holds the leg, to the operator.

(*c*) The pieces cut off the slaughtered animals, called in Egyptian *śtpwt* " The chosen "—haunches, rib-pieces, and hearts—are carried away *śḫp śtpwt*. One of the laden servants has the title of *ḫrp ìst* " [Controller of the registered] workmen ".

Pl. XXII, East Wall.

Above the door, offerings.

At the sides of the door, the bringing of the sacrificial animals.

Left : (1) *ìnt rn m'-ḥḏ* " The bringing of a young oryx antelope ". (2) A long-horned ox, which rubs its face with its hind foot. *śḫpt rn ìw' nt ìḫt-ḫ'wj* " Bringing a young ox for the evening meal ". (3) Hornless oxen. *śḫpt ḥrjw-db 'n Ḏḥwtjjt* " Bringing hornless oxen for the festival of Thoth ".

Right : (1) The same as on the left. (2) Hornless ox without inscription. (3) An ox with artificially bent horns *ìnt rn ìw'* " The bringing of a young ox."

Pl. XXIV. Niche.

The deceased seated, holding a whip, the symbol of authority. The inscriptions give his titles. In front of him on the ground sits his wife, *Ḫnwt*, Khenut.

Pl. XXIII. South Wall.

An exact counterpart of the north wall. The persons with inscriptions are :

First register. (*a*) " The gift to the ground ", as above, Pl. XXI.

Second register. (*a*) A "[Expert servant of the ka]" kneels on the ground, while a man standing behind him pours water on his hands, *rdjt mw* "Giving water".

(*b*) A offers incense *k'p śntr*. See Pl. XXI, first register, (*b*).

(*c*) The same as Pl. XXI, first register, (*b*).

(*d*) The same as Pl. XXI, first register, (*c*).

(*e*) offers incense

(*f*) Lector-priest. *ś'ḫt in ḫri-ḥb* "The glorifying" (of the dead who is proclaimed a spirit *'ḫ*) "by the lector-priest".

Third register. A man offering a goose.

Fourth register. (*a*) and (*b*) The two sons of the deceased, without gifts.

(*c*) *ḥm-k' mrr nb-f 'bdwj* "The [ka-servant], whom his lord loves, Abduy", bringing gifts.

(*d*) The other persons have no inscriptions, except a single man who is simply called .

Fifth register. (*a*) A bringing a goose. *śtp* "The choosing", i.e. To bring a sacrifice.

(*b*) A *imj-ḫt ḥmw-k'* offering incense.

Sixth register, beginning on the left.

(*a*) *int rn m'-ḥḏ* "Bringing a young oryx antelope".

(*b*) Butcher cutting off part of the hind-leg of an ox. *sfṯ ift*.

(*c*) A *śšmw* "Butcher", while cutting off the foreleg, says to his comrade who holds the leg, "Take".

(*d*) A man sharpening a knife *pḏt dś in śšmw*. See Pl. XXI, sixth register, (*b*).

(*e*) Slaughtered oryx antelope, *m'-ḥḏ*.

(*f*) Butcher eviscerating an animal. *šdt ḥ' tj*. "Taking out the heart."

(*g*) Same as (*d*).

(*h*) Same as (*c*).

(*i*) Same as (*d*), but without the words *in śšmw*.

(*j*) Man laden with a haunch waits for the heart, which is being removed from the carcass of the ox. He says, *imj ḥ'tj* "Give the heart".

(*k*) Man taking out the heart. See (*f*).

(*l*) Servant in working dress carries away the joints. *ḫrp iśt* "Leader of the workmen". Before him two others without inscription. Then like the first of the row.

(*m*)

(*n*) Title of the whole register: *śḫpt śtpwt* "Bringing the sacrificial joints".

23. Tomb of Shepses-Ptah I. Pls. XXV–XXVII.

Name. Read *Śpśś-Ptḥ* "Shepses-Ptah". A form like .

Titles.

(1) . See p. 11.

(2) *ni ḥb r'* "Belonging to the festival of the Sun", a title borne only by the High Priest of Memphis.

(3) *ḏb'tj* "[Sealer]".

(4) *ḥm-nṯr Ptḥ* "Prophet of Ptah".

(5) *ḥm-nṯr Skr* "Prophet of Seker".

Date. Vth dynasty.

Pl. XXVI. *Stele.* In the panel, the deceased before a table of offerings under which are the words, "thousands of bread, beer, cakes, oxen, oil, alabaster bowls (*šs't*), geese."

Below, the deceased standing, with his principal titles.

24. Tomb of Shepses-Ptah II. Pls. XXVIII–XXXI.

Name. See Shepses-Ptah I.

Titles.

1. See p. 11.
2. var. See Shepses-Ptah I.
3. See p. 12.
4. . See p. 14.

5. *ḥrj sšt' n . . . nṯr* "[Over the secrets of the sealer] of the God".

6. *ḫrp ḥmwt nbt* "[Controller] of every art".

7. *ḥnk ni-śwt*. See p. 12.

8. *w'b Ptḥ* "Priest of Ptah".

9. *imj-r pr Skr m iśwt-f nb* "[Intendant] of the House of Seker in all his places".

10. *ḥrj sšt' n nṯr-f* "[Over the secrets] of his God". Note: The spelling of *nṯr* with after the determinative is intended to show that it was still sounded before the suffix, though it was already lost, as in ⲛⲟⲩⲧⲉ.

11. . See p. 21.

12. *ḫrp śm* "[Controller of vegetables]".

13. *ḏb'tj* "[Sealer]".

14. *mrr nb-f* "He whom his lord loves".

15. "[Devoted to] the King".

16. "[Devoted to] Anubis".

17. "[Devoted to] Osiris".

18. "[Devoted to] his lord".

19. "[Devoted to] the great God, lord of the West".

20. "[Devoted to] Ptah."[1]

21. "[Devoted to] Osiris, lord of Busiris".

22. (var. with) "Deputy prophet of the pyramid, Dad-ysut, of Tety".

23. (var. with) "Deputy prophet of the pyramid, Nefer-ysut, of Unas".

Family.

1. Wife. *irjt-ḫ ni-śwt ḥmt-nṯr Ḥt-ḥr ḥmt-nṯr Nt* "The [courtier], prophetess of Hathor, prophetess of Neith, *im'ḫwt ḫr nṯr ''j, Intjt*. See p. 19.

2. Son. *imj-ḫt ḥmtjw Ś'bw* "[Pupil] of the workmen, Sabu". Pls. XXX, XXXI.

3. Son. Pl. XXX.

4. Son. Pl. XXIX.

5. Son. *ḫntj š pr-''j* "[The gardener] of Pharaoh".

6. Son. *Špśj pw Ptḥ* "Shepsy-pu-Ptah".

Servants.

1. *ḫrp sḥ Ḥtp-nj-Ptḥ*. See Pl. XXIX.

2. *imj-r k'r* (?) *N-św-Ptḥ*. "[Intendant] of clothing, Nisu-Ptah". Pl. XXIX.

3. *ḥm-k' Šdw-Ptḥ*. Pl. XXIX.

4. *imj-r iswt Mḥw* "[Intendant of registers] Mehu".

5. "[Intendant of clothing], Seshem-nefer". Pl. XXIX.

6. "[Intendant of works], Sebek-hotep". Pl. XXIX.

7. Pl. XXIX.

8. *imj-r . . . ir nwt Irj* "[Intendant of the linen], Yry".

9. "[Intendant of the registers], Nisu-Ptah". Pl. XXXI.

10. Pl. XXIX.

11. *sš pr dmḏt nṯr pr-''j Mn-iḫjj* "Scribe of the House of divine books

[1] Pls. XXIX, XXX, where the belongs both to *im'ḫw ḫr* and to Shepses-Ptah.

of Pharaoh, Men-ahy ". Men-ahy contains the name of Ahy, the little son of Hathor, Lady of Dendera.

PLS. XXX, XXXI.

12. *Nj-Ptḥ nfr ḥr*. PL. XXX.

13. *Śpdw-ḥtp*. PL. XXXI.

PL. XXXI. *Outer Walls*.

The deceased and his wife, with their titles and names.

Doorway. The deceased ; before him his son Sabu (see above, No. 2). Below, bearers of offerings, on the right without names, on the left Nos. 11 and 12.

Architrave. The left end only remains. *Ḥtp dj ni-śwt* formula, in which Osiris, Anubis and the Khenty-amentyu (*ḫntj-ỉmntjw*) are named. The wishes for the deceased are that he (may go upon the beautiful roads of the west) " on which " (the honoured ones go) " to the great God ".

PLS. XXIX, XXX.

The deceased sits in front of a table and a pile of offerings which are enumerated in a list. Funeral-priests and servants (for whose names, see above) bring him gifts. *m'' nḏt-ḥr ỉnwt m ḥtwt-f nwt-f nt t'-mḥ šm'* " Seeing the tribute brought from his towns and villages in Lower and Upper Egypt ".

On PL. XXIX in the topmost register an oryx antelope is being dismembered. " The dismembering of a young oryx ".

On PL. XXX, in the corresponding place, an ox is cut open. " The taking out of the heart ".

PL. XXVIII.

The False-door of the West Wall. Above : a *ḥtp dj nỉ'-śwt* formula in which offerings on all festival days are desired for the dead. Under the panel, in which the deceased sits before a table of offerings smelling a vase of ointment, there is a *ḥtp dj ni-śwt* formula wishing him a good burial.

On the outer columns at the sides of the stele there are, on both sides, the names of the seven sacred oils :

1. *śṯj-ḥb* " Festival perfume ".
2. *ḥknw*.
3. *śfṯ*.
4. *nỉ-ḫnm*.
5. *tw'wt*.
6. *ḥ'tt 'š* " Oil of cedar ".
7. *ḥ'tt ṯḥnw* " Libyan oil ".

CHAPTER VI.

25. TOMB OF SEKHEM-KAY. PL. VII.

The tomb of Sekhem-kay appears to have been entirely omitted in Professor Sethe's MS. I am therefore constrained to rectify that omission myself, which I do with some trepidation as my knowledge of the early periods is necessarily far below his.

Name. *Śḫm-k'-ỉ* " My ka is mighty ".

Titles.

1. *s'b ỉrj Nḫn n ḥt wr* " Judge belonging to Nekhen of the House of the Great One ".
2. *ḥrj šśt'* " He who is over the secrets ".
3. *ḥm-nṯr M''t* " Prophet of the goddess Maat ".
4. *ḥm-nṯr Śd* " Prophet of the god Sed ". This is a jackal god, of whom nothing is known.
5. *ḏ' m''t n nb-f* " True . . . of his lord ".
6. *wḏ-mdw m''* " Actual commander ".
7. *nj ḫrj ỉdbw* " Belonging to the overseer of lands ".
8. *ỉrj ḫ ni-śwt* " [Courtier] ".
9. *w'b ni-śwt* " Uab-priest of the King ".
10. *ỉm'ḫw ḫr nṯr* " Worthy before the great God ".
11. *mrj nb-f* " Beloved of his lord ".
12. *ḥm-nṯr Špśś (?) -k'-R'* " Prophet of Shepses-ka-Re' ". The middle sign of the cartouche is obliterated ; it is possible that it may be , not ; in which case the cartouche would be that of Dad-ka-Re'.
13. *ḥm-nṯr Ḥtḥr m ỉst ib* " Prophet of Hathor in the Place-of-the-Heart ". This is apparently the name of the obelisk of Hathor (*cf.* her name at Dendera).
14. *ḥm-nṯr N-wśr-R'* " Prophet of Ne-user-Re' ".

Family.

1. Wife. *ḥmt-f ỉmj-r ḥm-k' ỉrj ḫ ni-śwt Ḫnt-k'w-ś* " His wife, [Intendant of the servants of the ka, Courtier], Khenty-kau-es ". The name means " She who leads her kas ".
2. Son. *s'-f śmśw nb ỉm'ḫ s'b ś-ḥḏ sš w'b ni-śwt ỉrj ḫ ni-śwt Śḫm-k'-j nḏś* " His eldest son, lord of worthiness, [judge, expert scribe], uab-priest of the king, [courtier], Sekhem-ka-y, the younger " (lit. " the little ").
3. Son. *s'-f s'b sš Ḳ'j* " His son, the judge scribe, Qay ".

4. Daughter. *s't-f Ḫnnwt* "His daughter, Khenut".

5. Daughter. *s't-f Ỉntj* "His daughter, Ynty". It is tempting to see in these two daughters the wife of User-neter and the wife of Shepses-Ptah II. Unfortunately the identification cannot be proved.

6. Grandson. *s' s'-f Śḫm-k'-j* "The son of his son, Sekhem-ka-y.

Inscriptions.

Architrave. Three horizontal lines, of which the topmost is almost entirely obliterated. (1) "May the King give an offering . . . (2) May Anubis give an offering, Chief of the Hill of the Snake, He who is from the Oasis . . . (3) May Osiris give an offering, Leader of Dedu, funerary offerings for him on New Years' Day, on the festival of Thoth, on the First of the Year, on the festival of Uag, on the festival of Seker, on the Great Festival, on the (festival of the) Heat, and the going forth of Min".

False Door. Two horizontal lines along the top, of which the upper is almost entirely destroyed. (1) "May Osiris give an offering, the lord of Busiris". (2) "May the Gods of the necropolis give an offering." The name of Sekhem-kay is inscribed vertically across both lines at this point. Line 1 is obliterated, but line 2 continues: "Funeral offerings for him of bread and beer on New Year's Day . . . (on the festival of) Seker . . . on the Monthly festival and the two Half-monthly festivals". Crossing both lines vertically: "The uab-priest of the King, Sekhem-kay."

Central portion.

Panel. The deceased and his wife before a table of offerings. Their names and titles are almost completely obliterated. Above and to the right of the table is the list of offerings, ending with the dedication to "the judge, belonging to Nekhen, Sekhem-kay". Two horizontal lines of inscription below the panel: (1) "May the King give an offering, may Anubis give an offering, funeral offerings for him of bread and beer from the altar, on (the festivals of) the Month and the Half-month to the extent of eternity. (2) May be given to him grain from the Granary, clothing from the Treasury, pieces of meat . . . and a going forth among the worthy ones to the God." Crossing both lines vertically: "The judge, belonging to Nekhen, Sekhem-kay".

On each side of the panel is a scene. On the left the deceased is seated on a high-backed high-armed chair; he wears a wig of long straight locks, and holds in his right hand a fly-flap, in the left a short staff. At his feet sits his wife Khentyt-kau-es, her right arm embracing his legs. Under the chair his dog Pesesh (*Psš*) lies asleep, its nose on its paws, and the ribbons of its collar lying flat on its neck. On the right of the panel the deceased sits on a chair like that on the opposite side. He wears a short-curled wig; he holds a fly-flap in his left hand while his right is stretched out towards the offerings piled before him. Under his chair the dog Pesesh is awake, with head raised and the ribbons of its collar standing out from its neck.

Inner Jambs.

Left. The deceased standing, facing right. He wears a short-curled wig, and over his body is a conventionalised leopard skin. In his left hand he holds a long staff, in his right a cloth; above him are his titles and name. In front of him is a small figure of his eldest son, who grasps his father's staff. Above the son's head are his titles and name.

Below this scene is a register of five bearers of offerings:—

(1) *ḥm-k' Prnb* "The ka-servant, Perneb", holds up a jar. *mw (nm)śt* "Water libation, a *nemset*-jar".

(2) *ḥm-k' Śśk* "The ka-servant, Sesk", carries a demoiselle crane. *śḥp śtp* "Bringing the choice bird".

(3) *ḥm-k' Ttj* "The ka-servant, Tety", has a gazelle across his shoulders. *ỉṯt gḥs* "Carrying a gazelle".

(4) *ḥm-k' Ỉnn* "The ka-servant, Ynen" has a young hyaena in his arms. *ỉṯt ḥtt* "Carrying a female hyaena".

(5) *ḥm-k' Prḫw* "The ka-servant, Perkhu", has a goose of the kind called *ṯrp* "Therp", in his arms.

Right—The deceased standing, facing left. He wears a short beard and a skull-cap; in his right hand he holds a long staff, in his left a cloth; his titles and name are above his head. In front of him is a small figure of his wife with her titles and name above her. Standing between her and the long staff of Sekhem-kay is their younger son, Qay. He wears the lock of youth and holds fast to his father's staff. In the register below, five men bring offerings. The general title of the whole scene is *śḥpt pr-ḫrw* "The bringing of funerary offerings".

(1) *ḥm-k' Ỉpt* "The ka-servant, Ypet", bears a basin and ewer in one hand and a bird in the other.

(2) *ḥm-k' Înj* "The ka-servant, Yny", opens a censer, against which is the word *śnṯr* "Incense".

(3) *ḥm-k' Ḳdnś* "The ka-servant, Qednes", carries two pieces of cloth, *wnḫjw*.

(4) *ḥm-k' Ḫnw* "The ka-servant, Khenu", with a goose in his arms; *iṯt śrw* "Carrying a *seru*-goose".

(5) *nsj-b'st Nbw* "He who belongs to the vase, Nebu", carries a jar on his head. *int mw* "The bringing of water".

Outer Jambs.

These correspond with one another in arrangement. On each side are five registers. In the topmost are the family and friends; in the second and third are bearers of offerings; in the fourth and fifth are scenes of the sacrifice of oxen.

Left—(1) First (top) register. The seven figures represent Sekhem-kay's family, placed in the following order: Eldest son, younger son, two daughters, grandson, and two unnamed persons, possibly intended for young infants or even unborn children.

(2) The second register has five men bringing birds for the sacrifice. They are led by *śḥḏ ḥm-k' W'š-k'* "The [expert] ka-servant Uash-ka". The inscription of the whole scene reads *ḥr štp štpw m w'g Ḏḥwtj ibd ..nt m 'wt ḏt* "With the choicest of the choice on (the festivals of) Uag, Thoth, the Month and the Half-month to the extent of eternity".

(3) Five bearers of offerings, without inscriptions.

(4) Four butchers dismembering an ox. On the right the butcher Qednes says to his assistant *iṯt rk śšmw pw* "Pull thou, O butcher". On the left another butcher is skinning the animal; above him is the inscription *śfṯ iw'* "Cutting up the ox". The assistant is whetting his knife, *dm dś* "Sharpening the knife".

(5) In the lowest register are four men; two carry portions of the dismembered ox, *śḫpt štpw* "Bringing the choice pieces". The third man is removing the heart from the carcass, *šdt ḥ'tj* "The taking out of the heart". The unusual shape of the heart determinative should be noted. The fourth man is sharpening his knife.

Right—(1) Seven men in the attitude of respect with the left hand holding the right shoulder; their names and titles are given.

(*a*) *śn-ḏt w'b Mrj-m''t-nṯr* "The brother of eternity, the uab-priest, Mery-maāt-neter".

(*b*) *śn-ḏt s'b sš N-k'-'nḫ* "The brother of eternity, the judge scribe, Ni-ka-ankh".

(*c*) *sš' nï-śwt śḥḏ ḥm-k' 'nḫw* "Scribe of the accounts of the King, [expert] ka-servant, Ankhu".

(*d*) *sš pr-ḥḏ śḥḏ ḥm-k' Nj* "The scribe of the Treasury, [expert] ka-servant, Ny".

(*e*) *sš pr-ḥḏ śḥḏ ḥm-k' Ṯntj* "Scribe of the Treasury, [expert] ka-servant, Thenty".

(*f*) *s'b sš šḫt śḥḏ ḥm-k' Nfr* "The judge scribe of the fields, [expert] ka-servant, Nefer".

(*g*) *s'b sš Špśś-Ptḥ* "The judge scribe, Shepses-Ptah".

(2) Five men bearing offerings, of whom only the first is named: *śḫm sḥ Gw'* "The leader of the shrine, Gua".

(3) Five bearers of offerings, without inscription.

(4) Scene of sacrifice. General title: *śḫp štpw* "Bringing the choice pieces". The scene is presided over by *s'b sš Nfr* "The judge scribe, Nefer". He says to the butchers, *sfṯ ir sp* "Cut properly". Two men are removing the fore-leg of an ox; the chief butcher says to his assistant, who holds the leg, *iṯt rk* "Pull". Behind him another butcher holds a flint knife and a whetstone, *dm dś* "Sharpening a knife".

(5) The lowest register has another scene of sacrifice, without inscription.

CHAPTER VII.

DETAILS FROM THE TOMB OF TY.

26. PLATES II–VII. In STEINDORFF'S *Grab des Ti* the scale of reproduction is too small for the detail to be clearly seen; these figures are therefore published in a larger size, as they are among the finest examples of the skill of the Egyptian artist in depicting animals and birds. The references throughout this and the succeeding chapter are to Steindorff's publication.

PLATE II.—(*Ti*, ii, pl. 113.) The scene of a predatory animal climbing the reeds to attack a nest of fledgelings, and the mother bird flying to the rescue, is a common motive in Egyptian art, and occurs in most of the scenes of the marshes. Like all the best sculpture in the tomb of Ty, the artist of this scene, though greatly hampered by convention, has succeeded in introducing some dramatic touches. The catlike gliding motion of the mongoose along the papyrus stem, which bends beneath the weight, and the shivering terror of the little fledgelings, are well rendered. The adult bird, in this case a pintail duck, is entirely conventional in drawing ; its attitude does not suggest the impassioned speed of the despairing mother. One is therefore tempted to believe that the mother bird was done by another hand, possibly a journeyman sculptor who had not yet dared to go beyond the limits of pure convention in spite of his technical skill.

PLATE III (1). (*Ti*, ii, pl. 113.) The second representation of the tragedy of the marshes is neither so interesting nor so convincing as that on pl. xiv. The fluttered and screaming nestlings are less tragic than the silent and trembling little birds. The animal, which appears to be some kind of fox, is too heavy for the stem up which it is sedately walking. In comparing the two scenes, it is clear that they are by different artists. Though the technique is equally good in both scenes, the dramatic touch has been missed by the second artist, whose want of observation is shown by his placing the animal on the wrong part of the bent stem. The first artist very properly placed his animal on the horizontal part of the stem, where its footing would be secure, and the paws, which are not those of a climbing creature, would not be noticeably out of place.

So little is known about the artists who sculptured the tombs at Saqqara that it is always worth while to look for indications of individuality. The tomb of Ty, owing to its size and the extent of its decorated surfaces, is one of the most important for this purpose. In that mass of material it should be possible, by intensive study, to differentiate the work of the various artists.

(2) (*Ti*, ii, pl. 112). The scene of cattle crossing a canal under the charge of herdsmen is common in tombs of this period. The little procession is always headed by a calf carried on the back of one of the cow-herds, in this case a young boy. The little creature turns its head and calls in terror to its mother, who replies. The party are obviously nearing the bank for the water is not up to the knees of the calf-bearer, while the cows are still almost breast-deep.

27. PLATE IV, 1–10. (*Ti*, ii, pls. 112, 114, 115, 117, 118.) Details of offerings. Of these No. 1 (*Ti*, ii, p. 117) is important. It represents a shed where various kinds of food were prepared and then hung on a horizontal pole which is supported by posts. The two objects on the left are tied to a cord fastened to the pole and are not attached to the pole itself. The first of these objects is unexplainable ; the second is a fish split open and cleaned, ready for cooking. This is peculiarly interesting for the fish, like the ox head, was tabu as a food according to late texts and classical authors. Though fishing scenes abound, both as a sport for gentlemen and a livelihood for peasants, it is rare to find the representation of fish used as food (cf. PETRIE, *Medum.*, pl. xii). On the right hand side of the post four long narrow objects with square tips are suspended from a short bar which hangs from the pole ; they appear to be threaded on the bar from which they hang. Attached to the lower end of each of these objects is a similar object, smaller in size and with the end pointed, not unlike the hieroglyph of a dagger. I can offer no suggestion as to what these were intended to represent ; they may be some kind of vegetable prepared for cooking. Another group of four objects hanging alongside are, I think, root-vegetables peeled and scraped ready for boiling. A slender pointed pot sealed with a large cap of clay is the next object. Then comes a group of an earthenware stand filled with loaves (?), and flanked on either side by a globular vase, one of which hangs from the pole, the other from the stand. Next is an object like a thick sausage ; it is obviously soft for it is thinner in the middle where the suspension cord compresses it. A round object, a *pat*-cake perhaps, judging by the marks on it, has a hole in the middle through which the suspension cord passes. Below it hang four more of the root-vegetables. This is an important and interesting series for the study of food in the Old Kingdom.

11. (*Ti*, ii, pl. 115.) Two registers from one scene. In the upper register a dwarf leads a monkey larger than himself. He carries a stick carved at one end like an open hand ; this must have been for beating the monkey. The lower register shows a boy leading two hunting dogs. The curious distortion of the boy's right shoulder is apparently an attempt to portray a figure in profile ; similarly distorted figures occur several times in this tomb. Such artistic experiments are found occasionally in the Old Kingdom but are more common in the Middle Kingdom.

12. (*Ti*, ii, pl. 129.) The young ox, rather cruelly muzzled and tethered with too short a halter, is a good study of an animal almost full-grown yet retaining some of the aspects of an immature beast.

13. (*Ti*, ii, pl. 129.) The group of demoiselle cranes, herded together by a man at each side, is a fine example of the decorative effect beloved of the Egyptian artist. The central group of a single bird with a pair on either side is symmetrical, but the rest of the birds are diverse in attitude. The delicate outline and the exquisite detail make this little crowd of birds one of the most charming and delightful scenes in the whole tomb.

28. Plate V (1). (*Ti*, ii, pl. 112.) In the new-born calf the artist has been peculiarly successful in his rendering of the rounded forms and loose-jointed build of a very young animal.

2. (*Ti*, ii, pl. 112.) This animal is more conventionally rendered and has not the same youthful springiness of gait as the calf.

3. (*Ti*, ii, p. 115.) In the full-grown buck the hoofs show that the animal had always lived on the soft straw-strewn floor of the farmyard and had never had them hardened by the abrasive sand and rocks of the desert; it must have been bred in captivity. I have already pointed out (*Saq. Mast.* I, p. 13) that the little animals led by the farm women are miniature creatures specially bred by wealthy owners. In the series of three animals here given, the size is indicated by the new-born calf, the fawn is rather smaller, but the full-grown buck is only very slightly larger. The two young animals are tied by a twist of cord round the hind leg; the buck is more strongly secured by a double twist round the front leg.

5. (*Ti*, ii, pl. 118.) The little hedgehog in a cage is interesting, for the number of representations of this creature in Egyptian art is remarkable. In the Old Kingdom they appear in landscapes and, as here, as offerings; later, figures of hedgehogs are found, of blue faience in the Middle Kingdom, of other materials (usually pottery) in the New Kingdom; they are known as late as the Ptolemaic period. The animal was either very common or the peculiarities of its appearance and behaviour drew the attention of the artists. As it is so often included among the offerings of food-animals in the Old Kingdom, it must have been, like the hyaena (see *Saq. Mast.* I, p. 29), a food-animal whose use did not survive.

4. (*Ti*, ii, pl. 114.) A box-like crate of young ducks is also a common offering. The box was probably of osier or papyrus, the bars being omitted by the artist as confusing to the spectator and obscuring his view of the offering.

7, 8. (*Ti*, ii, pl. 129.) The two magnificent birds are finely differentiated in shape and markings. The *ḥap* is a rarer bird in the offerings than the *re*. The former is common in the hieroglyphs as the writing of the name of Hapi, one of the genii of the dead; but it does not occur in offerings after the Middle Kingdom. Here it is clearly the pintail duck. The *re* is the principal bird found in the offerings from the earliest to the latest periods. It was clearly a large handsome bird and popular as a denizen of the farmyard; it was probably more prolific and more easy to rear than the *ḥap*.

9. (*Ti*, ii, pl. 129.) The *pekhet* with its full crop is the origin of the *'ḳ* of the hieroglyphic script. The markings on the pinions distinguishes it from the other two birds. The distended crop appears to be its characteristic as a hieroglyph.

CHAPTER VIII.

HIEROGLYPHS FROM THE TOMB OF TY.

(*Plate numbers in brackets refer to Steindorff's "Grab des Ti".*)

29. Plates VI and VII. These special hieroglyphs from the tomb of Ty are published here as being either unusually fine examples or as showing some peculiarity. The greater number are too well known to need comment, and the notes therefore refer only to those which have some special interest. References are given only to the rarer signs.

1. (Pl. 133.) Read *yri*. The fillet and feather headdress are unusual. For the knobbed sticks and the beard, see *Saq. Mast.* I, pl. xxxvii, 3. In late writing the figure is often female.

2. (Pl. 48.) The ordinary determinative for a man. The beard is a rare feature in this sign.

3. (Pl. 71.) Read *yn*. This sign belongs almost entirely to the Old Kingdom.

4. (Pl. 125.) Read *f'*; it means "to carry", a combination of the determinative and the principal consonant of the word.

9. The alphabetic sign for *ḫ*. There used to be much uncertainty as to the meaning of this sign; it is now supposed to be the representation of the placenta (see Murray and Seligman, in *Man*, xi, pp. 165–171, in Borchardt, *Das Grab-denkmal des*

Sahu-re', ii, pp. 76–7. Also SETHE, *Dramatische Texte*, passim).

13. The hand with water pouring over it is the usual indication of the use of the ewer and basin among the offerings. The earliest examples of this group are on the stone bowls of the Ist dynasty.

31, 32. Read *ḏ*. This sign standing alone is the name of a king of the Ist dynasty; it then probably reads Wazti (*W'ḏtī*). It is the fetish or crest of the town of Aphroditopolis and is then represented with the feather of the west on its back, which seems to indicate that there was another snake-nome on the east side of the Nile. As the sacred object of Aphroditopolis it reads *w'ḏt*, which is the same as the cobra-goddess of the North. The creature must therefore be either the hooded cobra with the hood down, or that equally poisonous snake, the hoodless cobra, which is still known in Egypt.

41. The small vulture is the alphabetic sign '. This sign is generally called *aleph*, but the sound of the Arabic *aleph* would not account for its use in the transliteration of foreign words into Egyptian or for the various vowels which replace it in Greek and Coptic when Egyptian words are transliterated into those languages. I suggest that it stands for the sound called *hamza* in Arabic; any language which did not possess that sound would omit it in transliteration and use only the vowels which follow it.

47. (Pl. 125.) Read *ḫ'*. This is a composite group of the determinative and the principal consonant of the word.

56. Read *bd·t*. It is the name of one of Ty's farms, and consists of the usual town-sign surmounted by three ears of bearded wheat. The little bunch of three ears is found in STEINDORFF, *Grab des Ti*, pl. xliv, where it is held in a man's hand; and again in pl. cxxiv a reaper grasps a similar bunch, preparatory to cutting it off.

62, 63. (Pls. 85, 88.) Read *ḥn*. The divergence of form in this sign in early examples makes it one of the most interesting of the hieroglyphs. It always represents a young shoot, either flower bud or leaf bud, and the choice of the plant appears to have depended on the individual artist. Why the later scribes should have conventionalised it, in the form of one of the compositae, is not clear.

105. Read *šmś*. Late forms omit or alter the detail, and confusion has arisen in attempts to explain the true meaning. This example shows a heavy staff with a curved top; to the middle of the shaft a large packet is lashed, and the ends of the lashing project above and below the package. In some examples the upper end of the lashing is drawn like a knife, though it would be impossible to carry a knife or any other long narrow object at that angle. In late examples the lower end of the lashing is lengthened and drawn like a human leg and foot. [In this case it represents the follower carrying the hunting shield on his back, and holding the hunting knife. F. P.] As the sign is the determinative of the verb "to follow", it probably represents the equipment which a servant carried behind his master, perhaps when hunting.

114, 116. The development of the plough from the hoe is clearly seen in these two signs. The handle of the hoe elongated becomes the pole for yoking the draught animals, the blade becomes the ploughshare to which are attached the plough-handles for guiding it. The rope lashing of the two implements is exactly the same.

121. (Pl. 133.) Read *ḥm-t*. This sign is so commonly used as the word for "woman" that its origin is generally overlooked or forgotten, and it is therefore regarded as some kind of female organ. It is, however, also used as the determinative for "copper", and in detailed examples is always represented as being full of liquid. Its proper colour is blue, the invariable colour for copper in the hieroglyphs. It represents a crucible for melting copper. Crucibles are known from Badarian times, and though they sometimes have a spout to facilitate pouring they are often only plain circular pots. In this instance the thickness of the walls of the vessel and its long narrow shape show clearly that it was a crucible .

133. (Pl. 129.) A rare sign representing a plaited basket with a long handle ending in a knot.

141. Read *ḏr*. A charming example of the bunch of papyrus stems, cut into lengths and tied with a rope. Bundles of stems of this kind occur among the food offerings in the Old Kingdom, either lying in baskets or carried by offerers. The sign is used as the name of a king of the Ist dynasty, and is there the earliest example of a king being personally connected with the food supply. A later king of the same dynasty bears a name, Udy-mu, which again shows the idea of the king as connected with

fertility. Professor Petrie suggests that the bundle of stems represents flax, which would also indicate a reference to agriculture.

142, 144. Read *im'ḫ*. No real explanation of this sign is as yet forthcoming. The proper colour of it is red, which may mean wood or cloth. The structure of the object suggests wood, but the loop suggests thread or string. No example of the object in use has yet been found among the tomb scenes; it therefore remains among the unexplained hieroglyphs.

145. The sandal shows both toe-strap and ankle-strap. The ankle-strap does not appear to have been tied; it must have been a loose ring of leather over which the toe-strap was fastened. Sandals were common in the Old Kingdom. Still earlier they were probably part of the royal insignia which later became democratized. Nar-mer's sandals are carried by an attendant when he was in action. The earliest instance of sandals is the model pair in ivory of the predynastic period (PETRIE, *Diospolis Parva*, pl. x, 19, p. 22); they appear to be amulets.

148. (Pl. 129.) Read *ḥ'p*. This is one of the mysterious objects used in the ritual dances of the king. In the early examples it is not a true rectangle; here it is slightly obtuse, while in the ritual object in the XIIth Dynasty (PETRIE, *Koptos*, pl. ix) the angle is acute. It represents the corner-piece of a reed hut, and is a bundle of reeds lashed together and bent so as to form the angle-piece of the thatched roof where it joins the wall. Part of the thatch is shown lying over the angle-piece. The sign is used as both determinative and ideogram of *ḥ'p* "to conceal", an appropriate meaning for such a method of roof construction. Its use in ritual dances may refer to the king as a temple builder, and would thus bring him into connection with the goddess of building as well as the gods who possessed temples.

INDEX

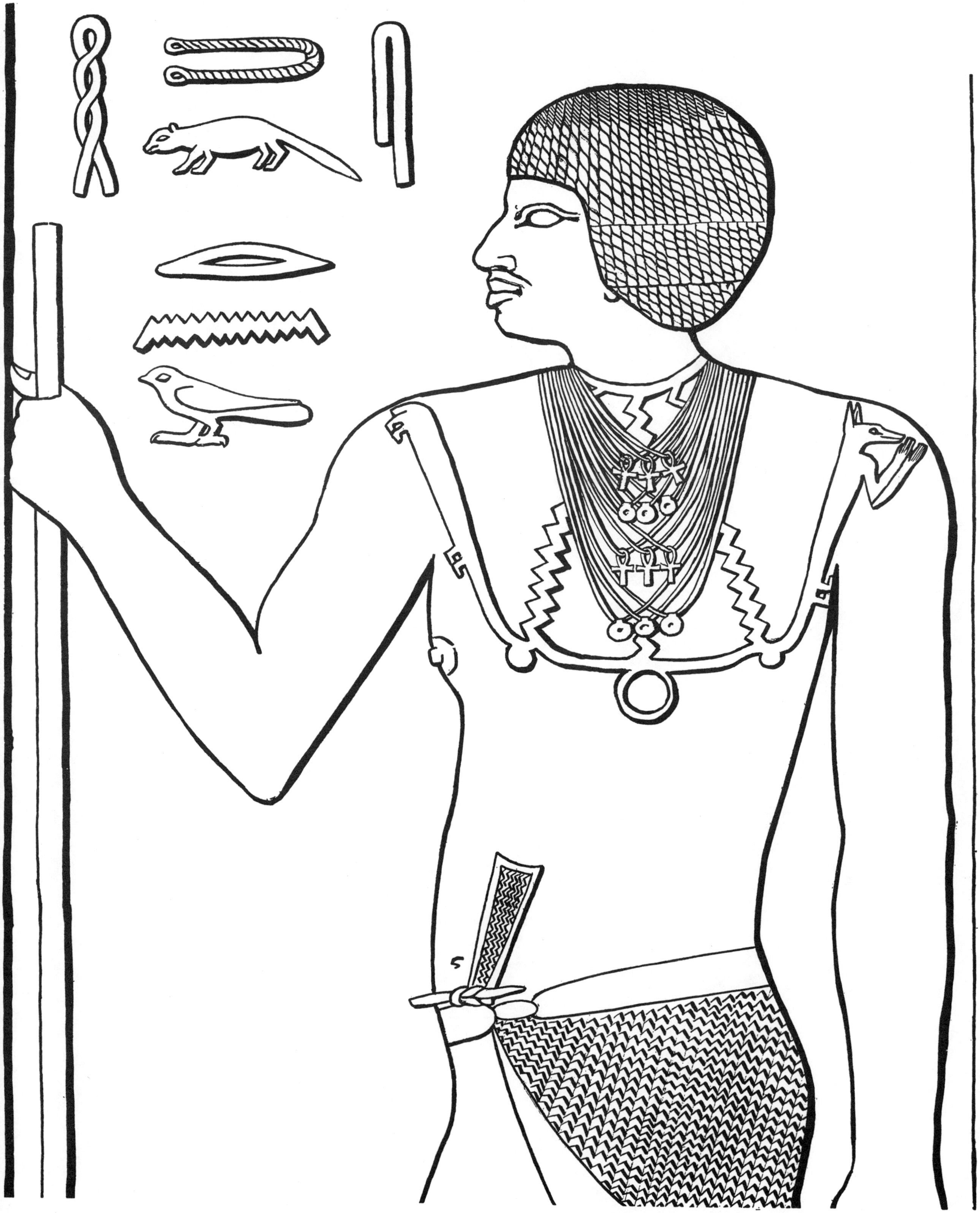

F. H.
M. A. M.

F. H.
H. P.

1

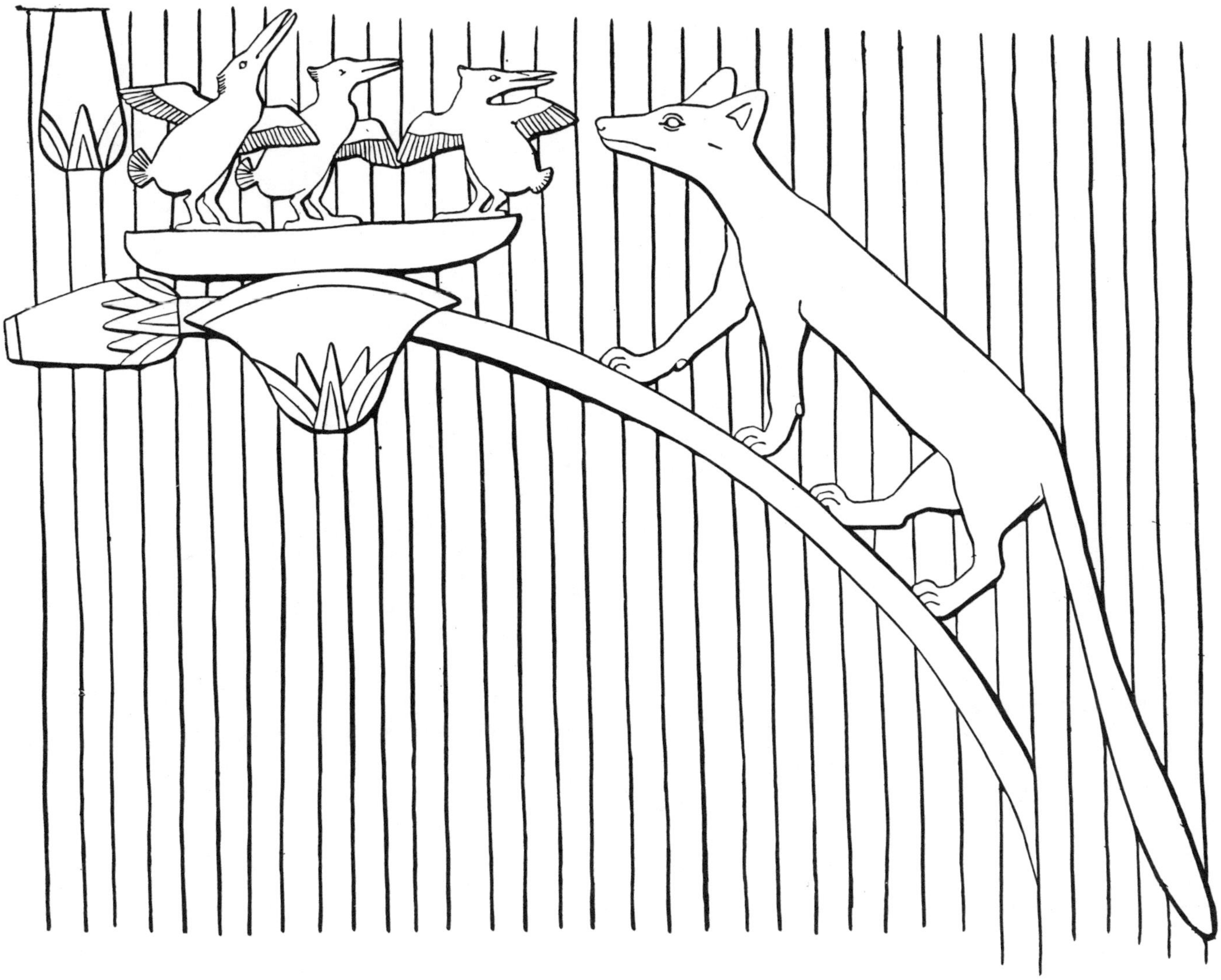

2

F. H.
F. K.
H. P.

F. H.
F. K.
H. P.

1

2

3
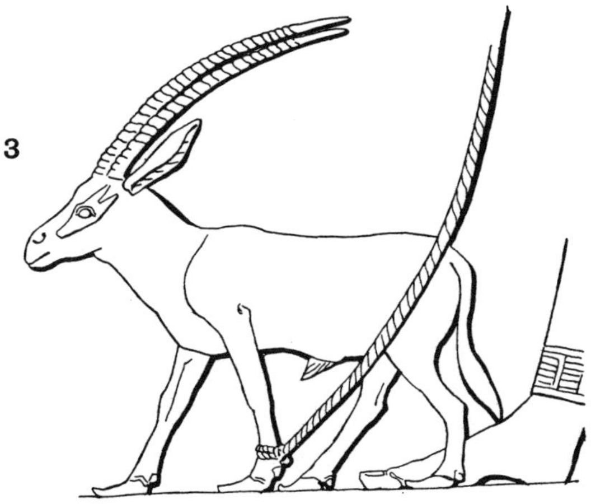

4

5

6
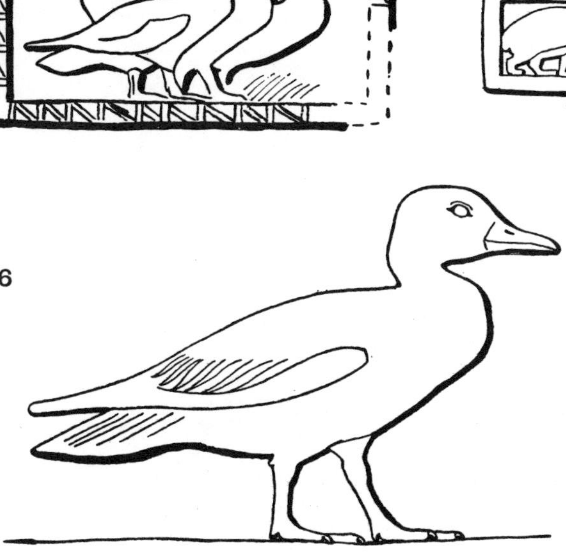

7

8

9
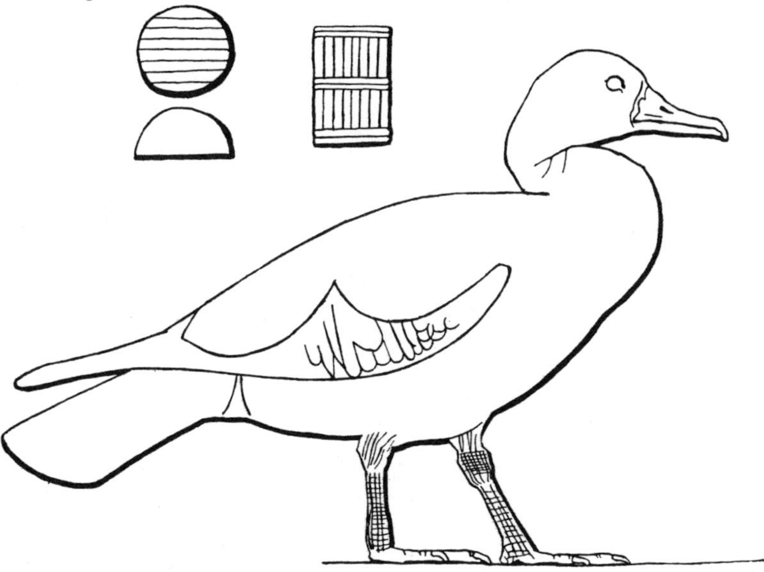

H. P.
F. H.
F. K.

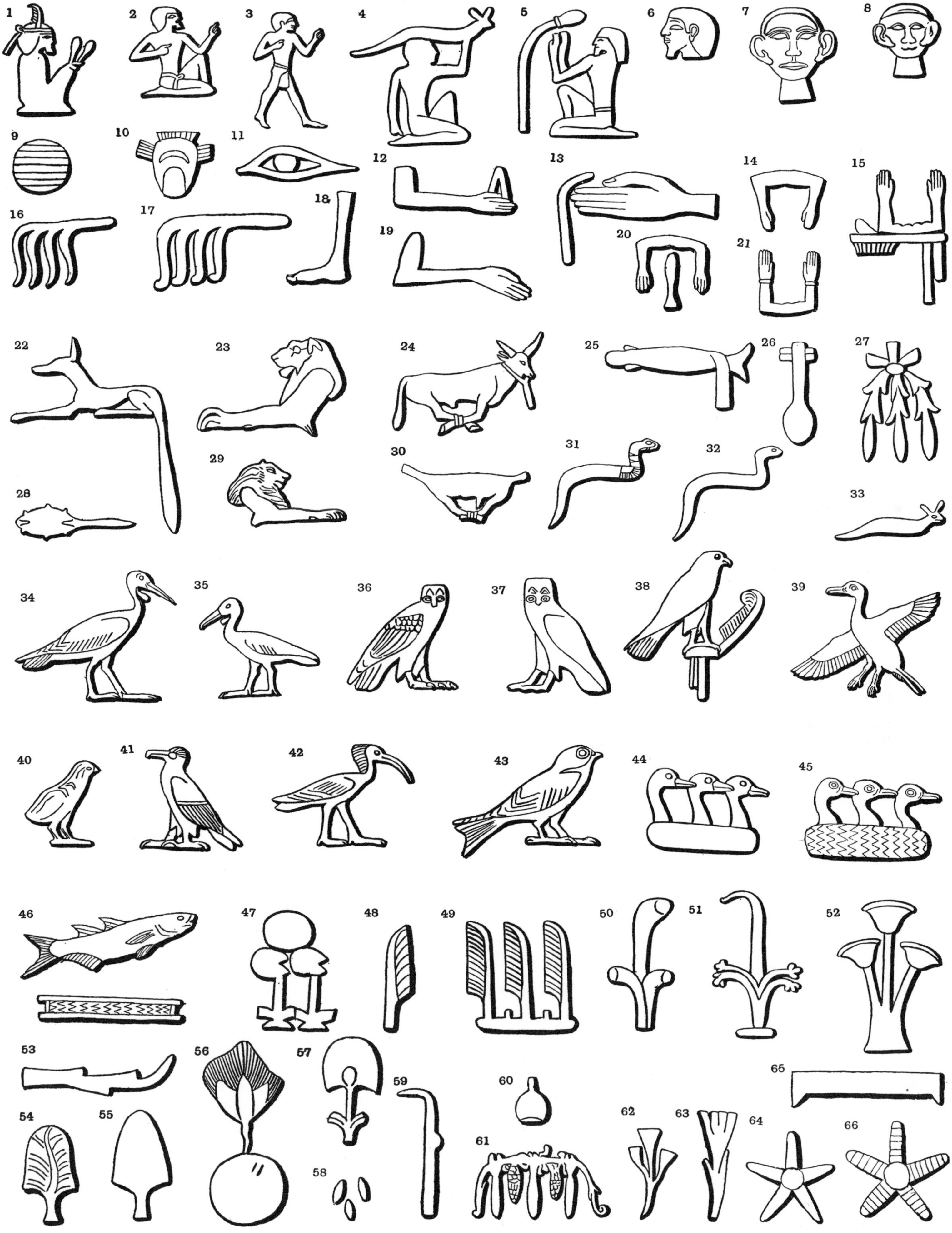
1
2
3
4
5
6
7
8
9
10
11
12
13
14
15
16
17
18
19
20
21
22
23
24
25
26
27
28
29
30
31
32
33
34
35
36
37
38
39
40
41
42
43
44
45
46
47
48
49
50
51
52
53
54
55
56
57
58
59
60
61
62
63
64
65
66

F. H.
F. K.
H. P.

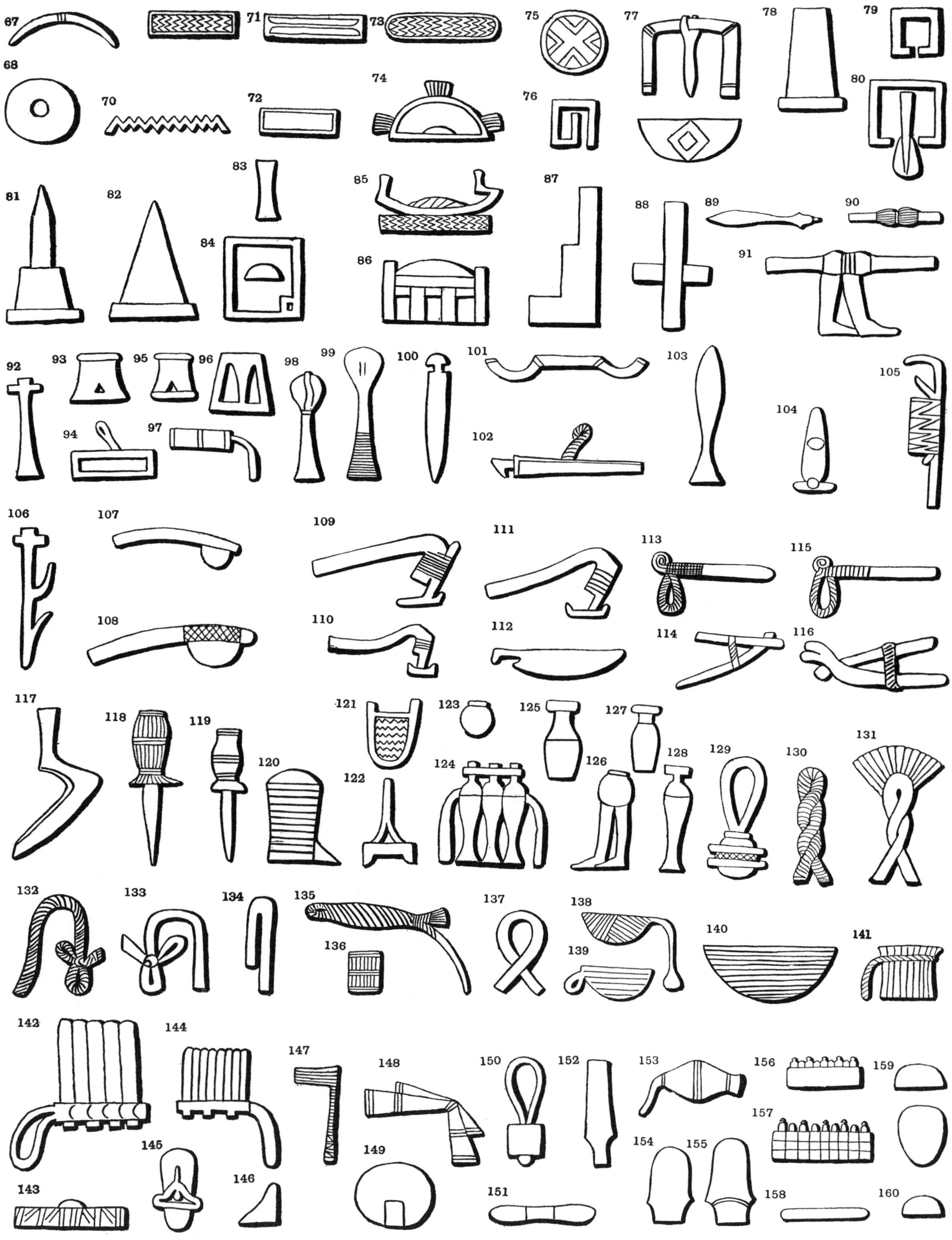
67
68
70
71
72
73
74
75
76
77
78
79
80
81
82
83
84
85
86
87
88
89
90
91
92
93
94
95
96
97
98
99
100
101
102
103
104
105
106
107
108
109
110
111
112
113
114
115
116
117
118
119
120
121
122
123
124
125
126
127
128
129
130
131
132
133
134
135
136
137
138
139
140
141
142
143
144
145
146
147
148
149
150
151
152
153
154
155
156
157
158
159
160

F. H.
F. K.
H. P.

III
IX, XII, XIII
XII
XXIII
XIV
VII
VII
VII
VII
XXXI
XXIX
X
XII
XVIII, XIX
XII
XXX
XVIII, XIX
VII
VII
VII
XI
XX-XXV
XXI, XXIII
VII
VII
IV, V
VIII-XVII
XI, XII, XIV
VI
XXIX
XXX, XXXI
VII
XXIX
VII
X
XXX

XXIX
VII
XII
VII
II
X
VII
XXIX
VII
XVII
IX
I
I, II
III
VII
VII
XXIV
VII
XXVII
XXX, XXXI
XXIX
XXXI
XI
VII
VII
VII
VII
X
XXIX
XXIX
VII
X
XXVI, XXVII
XXVII
XXVIII - XXXII
XXIX, XXX

XXIX
XXI, XXIII
VII
VII
XII
IX
III
III
X, XIV
VII
II
VII
VII

Royal Names

XII
IX
IX
XXIX, XXX
IX, XII
VII
XII
IX, XII
XXVIII-XXX
XII